Supernaturally Dysfunctional

S. E. Woody, ND

TRILOGY CHRISTIAN PUBLISHERS

TUSTIN, CA

Trilogy Christian Publishers
A Wholly Owned Subsidiary of Trinity Broadcasting Network
2442 Michelle Drive
Tustin, CA 92780

Supernaturally Dysfunctional

Rights Department, 2442 Michelle Drive, Tustin, CA 92780.

Trilogy Christian Publishing/TBN and colophon are trademarks of Trinity Broadcasting Network.

Cover design by: Beth Harp Photography, Lagrange, Indiana

For information about special discounts for bulk purchases, please contact Trilogy Christian Publishing.

Trilogy Disclaimer: The views and content expressed in this book are those of the author and may not necessarily reflect the views and doctrine of Trilogy Christian Publishing or the Trinity Broadcasting Network.

Manufactured in the United States of America

10 9 8 7 6 5 4 3 2 1

Library of Congress Cataloging-in-Publication Data is available.

ISBN: 978-1-63769-878-5

E-ISBN: 978-1-63769-879-2

Contents

Dedication

Thank you, Jon, the love of my life, for always believing in me.

Thank you, Mom and Dad, for always encouraging me.

Thank you to my children, who continually amaze and inspire me.

Thank you, friends and family, for the love, laughter, and necessary distractions.

Most of all, thank You, Jesus, for never giving up on me.

Foreword

I have had the privilege of being on earth for more than half a century and have lived in many different places around the world. While there are cultural differences wherever you go, humanity at the base level is the same. We all have fears, wants, insecurities, loves, hopes, and dreams.

In the backdrop of our lives, the influence of others hovers; sometimes our present family, sometimes ancestral, and sometimes people who come into our lives for a moment. When questioned, we often don't know why we do things a certain way or hold a particular idea to be true, and it's not until someone outside shines a light on these ideas and actions and exposes them that we question our past and come to the realization that we've unwittingly inherited the consequences of other people's actions and beliefs.

My good friend, Stephanie, is, in this book, shining a strong light on the demons of her past, and her own very human state of mind, and even more so on the redemption of Jesus and the incredible love God has for us. We are all human and come with *our own set of foibles; we are all puzzles to be pieced together and discovered over a lifetime. Stephanie does a masterful job of showing us the edges of our pieces while reassuring us that our dark sides are common to humanity and that God doesn't change the shape of the puzzle, but He can and does change the picture within it.*

It's my honor to introduce Stephanie to you, a woman I have known for years as honest, generous, and encouraging. We need Stephanie's warm words to remind us that in our dysfunction, we are loved and not alone. This book will undoubtedly touch your heart, make you think, and remind you of the redemptive love of God.

—Dr. Karen Workman
Certified Life Coach
Teacher, Public Speaker, and
Author of *Babysteps to Hollywood*

1

If the Dysfunction Fits, Embrace It!

I absolutely adore a good book! When you crack open that brand new binding only to find the words leaping off the page at you in such descriptive detailing that you are immediately whisked away into another world, unable to put it down. The house could be on fire, and you are so enchanted by the story unfolding between its pages that you don't even notice. Maybe a family member begins to interrupt your reading with a question or immediate need, and you shush them instantly. How dare they utter a sound at the very moment that Fabio whisks Alexandra away to Spain, saving her from a life of poverty and anguish! Alas, this is not that kind of book.

In all seriousness, this book has been in limbo for quite some time. The idea of it has ebbed and flowed in my mind throughout the past twenty years or so and has lately been continually on my heart. Maybe you are the reason for its timing. It is my prayer that whoever dares to glimpse at my first attempt at storytelling is blessed or touched by God in a new and exciting way.

My family and I currently reside in the Los Angeles area and have been deeply involved with the entertainment industry. You don't have to actually be a part of the industry, though, to notice that the paranormal, supernatural, or New Age phenomenon captured on film can usually guarantee millions of dollars to be made at the box office. Hollywood has made a fortune on haunted houses, demonic possessions, and ghostly or spiritual entity invasions. It seems as if there are new movies covering this subject matter practically every other weekend. What if I were to tell you that these scary movie themes were partially true? Maybe not in the way that we view it on the big screen, but more so the supernatural influences that surround us today. Skeptical? I don't blame you. If I hadn't lived through it myself or witnessed some of it first-hand, I would undoubtedly be feeling the same.

Just as there are both good and bad people in the world today, there are also positive and negative supernatural influences that can envelop an individual or family. In some instances, the negative influences may be largely or partly due to generational curses, as would seem to be the case in my own family. My descendants factually include, but are not limited to, mediums, successful suicides and suicidal attempters, verbal and physical abusers, demonic possessions, witches, and bootleggers, just to name a few. Though this may sound like a Halloween party rolled up into a nightmare, believe me when I tell you that this is in no way an exaggeration. I'm relatively certain that a few of these examples would most definitely belong on the cursed side of the family tree. It's not entirely all doom and gloom, however. Curses can be broken, wounds can mend, and lives can be forever changed, despite the trail of carnage that drags along behind them.

Before taking you all the way back in time to weave my tale of woe, I should probably warn you; it isn't a pretty ride. My family, overall, purposefully does their best to keep life interesting. By now, I'm sure that you've heard the ever-popular twenty-first century saying, "Our family put the 'fun' in dysfunctional." I'm living proof that it's true, and I'm not ashamed to share it. My roots run deep into the hills of Virginia, where my mother was born. So many things endear me to the south and its people. One favorite unspoken tradition, in particular, includes the fact that they don't try to hide their crazy family members. Rather, they parade them out on the front porch, sweet tea in hand, for all the world to see. Some people in other areas of the country may put on a façade that they are completely normal and try to repress the crazy gene at all costs, but what fun is that? My family loves to laugh out loud, speak their minds and endlessly tease each other.

All kidding aside, I'm pretty sure that most families are dysfunctional in varying degrees because all human beings are flawed. No one on earth is perfect, and life can get messy. Left untreated, major dysfunction may often leave deep wounds that could, unfortunately, take a lifetime to mend.

The dictionary[1] defines dysfunctional as "not operating normally or properly: behaving or acting outside social norms." The definition of it really doesn't sound too terribly bad. In fact, it could describe me on any given day for any number of reasons. Who really wants to be normal anyway? I believe a main character from one of my youngest daughter's favorite Halloween movies said it best, as she stated that being normal is vastly overrated. I remain in total agreement with that statement.

My family is far from normal. Most likely, yours is too. That's part of what makes us unique in this world. The Bible tells us in Matthew 5:13, "You are the salt of the earth. But if the salt loses its saltiness, how can it be made salty again? It is no longer good for anything except to be thrown out and trampled by men." We are the seasoning or flavoring on the earth today. I'm convinced that above average, beyond normal people, are the salt of the earth. I equate normal with being bland and flavorless. The exact opposite of what the Bible says we should strive to be like.

---

1 www.dictionary.com

2

Biblically
Dysfunctional

Salty, dysfunctional families have been around since the beginning of man on earth. Most of us are familiar with the very first family in the Bible. In chapter 3 of the book of Genesis, we are told how Eve persuaded her husband, Adam, to go against God by eating from the tree of forbidden fruit. When God asked Adam about it, he blamed his wife for giving it to him, while Eve, in turn, blamed the serpent. Let the record show that no one forced Adam to eat the fruit. He chose to be disobedient, as did his adoring wife. I also find it interesting that they didn't instantly own up to what they had done and were all too eager to let someone else take the fall for their mistake. At present, the blame-game mentality also appears to be a recurring theme for the political climate of our nation. This is obviously nothing new as its very origins were in the Garden of Eden. You'd think we would have learned our lesson by now.

Moving down to chapter 4 in Genesis, we learn about Cain and Abel, the sons of Adam and Eve. We know that Abel was a shepherd while his brother Cain farmed the land. The chapter goes on to explain that God was extremely pleased with Abel's sacrifice, which was the firstborn sheep of his flock. God was less than thrilled with Cain's offering of fruits from his own garden. As the story unfolds, we discover that this didn't sit well with Cain, who, in a jealous rage, killed his own brother and then lied to God about it.

The very first family on the planet exemplifies the qualities of dysfunction, and then some. Through them, we uncover the very first signs of deception, envy, and murder within the human race. Adam's family is not the only one in biblical history to have been known for greatly missing their mark as a healthy, thriving, and functional family. They just have the high honor of being the first ones to have their numerous dysfunctions recorded, in the number one best-selling book of all time, adding insult to injury. I mean, if the very first family had dysfunctional issues right out of the gate, there has got to be hope for the rest of us, right? Way to go, Adam!

In chapter 9 of Genesis, beginning with verse 18, we learn about Noah's dysfunctional life after he and his family were finally able to exit the ark onto dry land. It makes a great deal of sense to me, personally, that in celebration of all that he and his family had endured during the flood and the lives that were saved, he felt it necessary to plant a vineyard. The story takes a twisted turn in the chapter as he celebrated a little more than he should have, over-served himself in the wine department, and passed out buck-naked in his tent. An understandably easy thing to do, as the origin of this writing attempt, occurred during the time of COVID-19 and lockdowns galore. If a worldwide pandemic could lead to the occasional abuse of alcohol, I am sure that being cooped up in an ark for forty days and nights along with your family, literally tons of animals, with the boat continually rocking and no end in sight, could quite possibly be an enormous cause for the celebration of the century upon a final arrival on dry land! Am I alone here? Well, there may be more than a few of us who could relate to Noah's antics and outcome, especially at this point in our country's very own history. Though, naked in a tent would be interesting to try to explain away even today, during Noah's time, that alone would have been deemed disgraceful. Especially since he was a devout man of God, having great favor with him along with undoubtedly being the head of his own family. When his son, Ham, found Noah passed out in the tent, he ridiculed him, ran out to tell his brothers, and most likely anyone else who would listen. This respectable man of God messed up, and his loving son left him in a shameful, naked state instead of covering him up and keeping the entire event to himself. I guess in Ham's defense, the whole "honor thy father and mother" thing hadn't been written in stone at that time, but I'm sure it was an expectation.

We don't have to move ahead very far in the Bible before we find a few issues with Abraham and his wife, Sarah. In Genesis 12, beginning in verse 10, we discover the happy couple in Egypt, most likely traveling among some people known for killing husbands and taking wives whenever they felt like it. No disrespect intended for the future father of our faith, but it would seem a major cowardly move for Abraham to instruct his wife to tell strangers that she and Abraham were siblings instead of being married. He was obviously doing this to save his own life. I'm not convinced that he was thinking of Sarah at all on this one. History has shown that this was not the only bright idea that Abraham and Sarah concocted merely to have it backfire in the end. Even though Sarah was in her seventies, she was still very beautiful, according to the scripture. The Pharaoh of the land took an immediate liking to Sarah and added her to his harem. The Bible isn't clear on the exact amount of time that Sarah was in the palace before God infected the Pharaoh with serious illnesses. When it had become evident to Pharaoh that Abraham had fooled him, he released Sarah, allowing them both to safely leave his kingdom. Abraham, known throughout the Bible as a man of great faith, had lied.

When moving on to chapter 16 of Genesis, we read that Abraham and Sarah had yet another wonderful idea. Since God had promised them offspring as numerous as the stars, and since they were very old and couldn't imagine it happening the old-fashioned way, they decided to take matters into their own hands. You remember the story. Sarah gave her maidservant, Hagar, to her husband, and they conceived a child. Though hard to believe, things didn't turn out entirely the way Sarah had hoped. Hagar began to look down on Sarah and undoubtedly flaunted the fact that she bore Abraham's son while Sarah remained barren. Sarah started to mistreat Hagar, then blamed Abraham for the entire mess. Abraham ultimately had to send Hagar and his only child away in order to keep the peace with his wife, Sarah. Perhaps Abraham and Sarah could have coined the phrase "happy wife, happy life," though they were far from the definition of being one big happy family.

Genesis 19 includes the story of Abraham's nephew, Lot, who was living with his family in Sodom and Gomorrah. When the men of the city wanted to engage in intercourse with the angels who were visiting Lot's home, what did this loving and wonderful father decide would be the best course of action to take to appease the restless crowd of men surrounding his house? He did the unthinkable. He offered his two virgin daughters to the men instead. I must admit it is extremely difficult to wrap my head around that hyper-dysfunctional conclusion as well.

But Lot's notorious nonadaptive exploits didn't end there. It continued long after he and his daughters escaped the destruction of Sodom and Gomorrah. Since there were no men around for them to marry at the time, the daughters got their father drunk for two consecutive nights, slept with him, and became pregnant. Undoubtedly, on all accounts, a morally unwise decision. Though it would seem Lot himself may have paved the way for this scenario to play itself out when he quickly offered up his own daughters to be raped or murdered at the hands of an angry and evil-intending mob of men pounding on the door of his home. Just knowing that your father, who was designed by the Lord to protect and love you, could so easily ruin your life at the drop of a hat might just make you more inclined to come up with such a devious plan.

Let's move on to the life of Isaac, Abraham's son. When he was getting old with failing eyesight in Genesis 27, Isaac sent for his first-born son, Esau, to give him a special blessing before he died. While Esau was out hunting, his mother, Rebekah, devised a plot with her favorite son, Jacob, to steal the first-born son's birthright by deceiving Isaac. Their plan inevitably worked. When Esau found out about it, he threatened to kill his brother, Jacob, who then ran away to stay with his Uncle Laban. If you're keeping score here, Isaac's beloved wife, Rebekah, was in on the deception and actually pitted her own two sons against each other.

Don't worry; the family fun didn't end there. Uncle Laban ended up tricking his nephew, Jacob, who had just recently deceived his slightly older brother. Jacob fell in love with Laban's beautiful younger daughter, Rachel. He worked seven years for his uncle in order to marry her. The morning after the wedding finally took place, Jacob woke up to find he had been tricked into marrying Leah, Laban's older daughter, instead of Rachel. Jacob then went on to work for his uncle another seven years and was finally granted Rachel's hand in marriage. Jacob, a deceiver himself, was deceived by his uncle, who had now become his father-in-law. We could go so far as to say that he did indeed reap what he had sown, though in this case, he left a few casualties and hurt feelings along the way. Leah, knowing she had not even been Jacob's first choice as a bride, was not as pretty as her younger sister and spent much of her life vying for his affection. This doesn't sound like a happy or even healthy functioning family, in my opinion. I can't even begin to imagine what their holiday celebrations or dinners may have been like.

We just can't exit the book of Genesis without a little more of a discussion about Jacob, now known as Israel, and his sons beginning in chapter 37. I guess, since Jacob himself was his mother's favorite child, it would make sense that he had a preferred son as well. Jacob flaunted his love for Joseph by giving him a richly ornamented coat of many colors, which Joseph paraded in front of his already jealous older brothers. Joseph also made the mistake of telling them about a dream he had in which his brothers would one day bow before him. Filled with anger, the brothers decided to kill Joseph and throw him into a pit. One of Joseph's brothers, Reuben, talked the others into only putting Joseph into the pit instead of killing him. He planned to go and rescue Joseph while his brothers were away. Reuben returned to the pit and discovered that his brothers had already sold Joseph to the Ishmaelites, who took him on to Egypt. They took and tore Joseph's robe, covered it in goat's blood, and told their father, Jacob (Israel), that Joseph had been killed. This story represents the very definition of "brotherly love" and dysfunction at its best.

The Bible tells us in Numbers 12:3, "Now Moses was a very humble man, more humble than anyone else on the face of the earth." Even Moses, who was known for being humble in spirit, had a bad temper. In Exodus 2:11 and 12, we find it recorded that he killed an Egyptian who had been beating a Hebrew worker. Moses had, at that time in history, discovered he was Hebrew as well and could no longer stand to see someone of his own heritage being severely hurt at the hand of an Egyptian. Even though Moses had a rough beginning, given up as a baby, adopted into an Egyptian palace, and even killed an Egyptian, he still had a great purpose and an amazing life. Moses murdered someone, was totally forgiven, and then used by the Lord to perform miraculous signs and wonders. He was undoubtedly spiritually conflicted at times, which could inevitably exemplify the very definition of dysfunction in and of itself.

In 1 Samuel chapter 18, we learn that Israel's first king, King Saul, grew angry when returning home from the battlefield after David had killed Goliath. Many women gathered to meet the king and his men, celebrating their victory, and were singing in verse 7, "Saul has slain his thousands, and David his tens of thousands." The people seemed to love David more than the king, which fueled King Saul's hatred even more. At that point, the king decided to have David killed. The king's son, Jonathan, who loved David like a brother, helped him hide from his vindictive father. This ultimately led to disharmony, or dysfunction, in King Saul's family since he then practically disowned his son.

Moving on to 2 Samuel in chapter 11, we learn about David, "a man after God's own heart" (Acts 13:22), who committed adultery with Bathsheba. When she became pregnant, to cover up his own sin, David had Bathsheba's husband killed and took her as his wife. Later in chapter 15, we read about how David's own son, Absalom, betrayed him. Obviously, David himself made some selfishly dysfunctional decisions that caused a trickle-down effect, causing family drama and possibly a family curse or two. David had an incestuous son who raped his sister and another son who had that very brother killed for his actions. Absalom, who killed his brother, also desired to take over his father's throne. Through it all, David continually relied on and gave thanks, honor, and praise to the Lord. He will always be remembered as being "a man after God's own heart" in the eyes of the Father. A pretty good legacy, considering the messes and challenges he faced. One worthy enough to be mentioned in the ancestral lineage of Jesus. So, to share a line from one of my favorite classic movies, David has "got that going for him, which is nice."

In 1 Kings chapter 11, we discover that King Solomon, the wisest man who ever lived, had 700 wives and 300 concubines. Just for himself. God had told him not to intermarry so that he wouldn't be influenced by the gods that his many wives worshipped. Solomon didn't listen to God and married them anyway. His wives succeeded in turning his heart away from the Lord and towards their gods instead. God raised many adversaries against the king. In 1 Kings 11:11, we learn that God told

Solomon, "Since this is your attitude and you have not kept my covenant and my decrees, which I commanded you, I will most certainly tear the kingdom away from you and give it to one of your subordinates." One thing that we can be absolutely sure of, without a doubt, is that God will always do what He has promised.

Jesus's earthly family was somewhat dysfunctional as well. According to Luke 2:41-51, his very own parents left him, a twelve-year-old child, behind in Jerusalem while they traveled back toward their home. They didn't even discover him missing for three whole days. It's especially hard to understand that no one even noticed he wasn't in the caravan before leaving Jerusalem. Didn't they believe in head counts before setting out, as many large families do? Jesus was undoubtedly special, the chosen one, even though He was a child. This story baffles me as a mom who hovered over her children continually, with mama bear precision, to ensure their safety. I guess it makes for a better story that even Jesus' parents missed the mark occasionally. Not only that, but can you imagine how challenging it would have been for Joseph, as Jesus's stepfather, to challenge, correct, or reprimand the Lord as a small child? In my opinion, Joseph deserves more than a medal or honorable mention. He had to have been a very uniquely special individual.

These few examples show us that God often uses broken or cracked vessels to do His will and further His kingdom. Most of these people were dysfunctional in one way or another, but all were used by God as described in the Bible, and all had a specific purpose and destiny. They were flawed human beings, and many still did great and amazing things for the Lord. In turn, we have received some wonderful life lessons from them all. There is substantial proof in these very passages that even though we all have varying degrees of dysfunctionality, God can still use us to bless others and further His agenda.

Believe it or not, this is where my story begins.

3

Home-Grown Dysfunction

My mother, Lucy Anne, never really had a childhood. She grew up in an extremely small southern town with eight other siblings, an abusive alcoholic father, and a mother who was continually struggling to manage each day without angering her husband. They grew their own food, made all their clothes, and worked at early ages to try to earn some money. My mom began working at the age of eleven years old. When she talks about her past, she will often remark that she never got to be a little girl, which is gut-wrenching, to say the least. To me, this clearly explains much about her choices and unbreakable spirit of survival. My grandfather barely supported his family, and my grandmother never told her children that she loved them. The children grew up woefully neglected, feeling unwanted and unloved. Most siblings moved out early and married young, just to get away from home.

As the story goes, Lucy Anne got married at the age of eighteen to an older man. I was born around nine months later, in the December of 1967. During her pregnancy, and while my biological father served in the Vietnam War, she stayed with her sister, Willow, and her second husband, Denny. My mother and aunt shared countless stories throughout my childhood about how my uncle Denny continually told my mom that the little girl she was carrying would be his daughter too, whenever I finally decided to make my appearance. He and Aunt Willow already had three little boys, filling their home with laughter and mischievous chaos. I'm grateful to them for all the love, care, and support my mother was given during this crucial time in her life. I guess my uncle loved me before I was even born and just knew I would be a girl. But as fate would have it, and as my mother's belly grew, Uncle Denny, an officer in the army, was called back into duty. He never made it home. He was injured and put in a hospital that was later attacked by the enemy. To this day, I feel a very strong connection to Uncle Denny and have seen him several times in my dreams. The bond I've always felt to the uncle I've never met in this world is so strong that my youngest child even bears his name.

My biological father returned physically from the war to his little family, but never mentally. In his own way, I'm sure he believed he did the best that he could to forget all that he had gone through in Vietnam. He definitely brought it home to my mother and me. He no longer wanted the responsibility of a wife and child, and it showed as my mom spent most of their married life in tears and torment until their divorce. Her weight dropped sharply down to a mere ninety-seven pounds when her doctor told her that if she didn't start eating, her baby girl would soon be motherless. I am here today because she listened. I used to wonder if that was why I was put on the planet: to give my mom a reason to live at a time when God knew she needed one.

A few years later, my mother re-married. Estel came with three little boys of his own, and no, we were absolutely nothing at all like "The Brady Bunch." (And we all know how well that family turned out, don't we?) To a three-year-old, he looked like a cross between Elvis and Johnny Cash, my mom's favorite singer. After the wedding, my biological father, who had abandoned Mom and me, asked my new stepfather to adopt me. I'm pretty sure he no longer wanted the financial responsibility of paying child support. He no longer wanted me. But Estel did. I'm the special gift with purchase included with my beautiful mother. I did sometimes wonder while growing up if Estel adopted me because he wanted me, felt sorry for me since my real father wanted nothing more to do with me, or did he just feel he had to since he and my mother were now married?

Can you guess what this does to the psyche of a little girl growing up knowing all along that her biological father didn't want her and made her mother miserable, almost causing the end of her life? Well, I can tell you that it's not all lollipops and rainbows and not something that is easily dismissed. It's embedded in your mind and rears its ugly head every now and then in messed up, mysterious, and often haunting ways.

I should also share that my new dad, the only dad I've ever truly known, loved me so well that I rarely ever thought about my biological one. I was chosen and loved, regardless of his motives at the time. God showed up and saved my mother and me. As an added bonus, my dad came with three little boys that weren't very happy to have a new little sister. Let the dysfunctional games begin!

The disdain my new brothers held for the less than welcomed new ladies of the house was blatantly obvious and evident at most family gatherings. As a very little girl, I must admit that I wasn't aware of the fact that they didn't like me or hated my mother and blamed her for the divorce of their mom and dad. This was a lie that my brothers believed for decades, up until Dad heard one of them mention it in conversation, not so very long ago. He let them know, in no uncertain terms, that he and their mother had divorced years before he had ever even met mine.

It had taken my dad quite a while to get my mom to go out with him in the beginning. I'm sure this had much to do with the way my biological father had mistreated her and the main reason she was so hesitant to let another man into her life. Try to explain that scenario to little boys who, from very young ages, were told a lie that they believed to be true. The longer the mind dwells on a certain point, whether true or false, the truer the story appears to be for that specific individual. It then becomes his own personal truth. He will believe it with every fiber of his being. Once believed to that extent, no one could ever sway an opinion or change that very belief, regardless of the facts presented or proven timeline of events. This led to endless battles, trials, testing, and hate-filled family adventures. Party on!

An anonymous individual once coined the phrase that hindsight is twenty-twenty, and rightly so. I often wonder if my mother had known all she would have to deal with in our family and had the chance to do it all over again, would she take a quick pass, at warped speed, and say a polite "no thank you"? Believe me, there are times when I sincerely wouldn't have blamed her a bit if she had or even entertained the thought of bailing.

My dad was allowed to have his boys two days a week back then, and on some holidays and vacations, but never on Christmas. That's how and when our traditional Christmas Eve celebration began, which is still followed to this very day. Our family made the most out of our time together. Dad did everything he could to keep the family peace, which in and of itself was a full-time job.

As in most families, when the children get older, the conflicts get bigger and are often more difficult to resolve. More than once, my brothers, sister, or I have made life, well, I'll just say it, a living hell for our parents. I am truly surprised that they made it through raising us without divorcing or flat out killing one of us and just telling God we died, knowing he would have understood completely. Next year will be their fiftieth wedding anniversary. I'm sure their strong faith and genuine love for each other mended wounded hearts, allowing them to unconditionally forgive their little brood of stubborn, rebellious, and otherwise overtly obnoxious antagonists. And for the record, though sad to admit, this is no exaggeration. Any one of my siblings would agree with the above-mentioned statements, though we would squabble about who gave Mom and Dad more sleepless nights, the biggest headaches, or their grey hair. I think I may be tied for second place.

4

A Medium Among Us

From the moment of my birth, I've always adored my aunt Willow. I slept over at her home many times. My aunt would always tell me that even as a baby, I would listen to her better than my own mother. I believe that when I was tiny, my mom and aunt very closely resembled each other, which could explain why I listened so well to her. Or perhaps it was due to the sweet southern charm she oozed as she spoke gently with a little drawl that lulled you comfortably into her world and made you feel important as well as loved.

An interesting memory that sometimes surfaces had to do with one specific weekend. I was a very little girl at the time but can recall the events as if they just happened yesterday. I remember waking several times in the middle of the night and witnessed a few strange things in her room. I noticed small red orbs of light shoot across the ceiling of the bedroom, or at times appear to be dancing around it. The orbs seemed to just hover above the bed or in a corner as the evening dragged on. At some point in the middle of the night, I thought I saw a mass forming in the corner of her room. As it came more clearly into focus, it looked like a little girl with long blonde hair. I remember as a little girl myself thinking that I was dreaming and needed to go to sleep. I'm sure I was afraid, though I don't know why I never spoke of what I thought I had seen at the time. The girl just stood there, staring at me, without moving or uttering a sound.

The very next day, my aunt was going to take me to the church she had been attending when her boyfriend persuaded her to take me to the beach instead. It wasn't until much later that we discovered my aunt had belonged to a spiritualist church and that she was, in fact, a practicing medium. In case you are wondering, a spiritualist church service is usually conducted by a medium, someone who mediates communication between the spirits of the dead and the living. It usually involves some type of demonstration of mediumship and often includes a formal healing circle towards the end of their service.

Most mediums believe they have a personal spirit guide to contact for worldly as well as spiritual guidance. My aunt even, coincidentally, found a painting of her very own "spiritual Indian guide," the one who had been continually appearing to her. The painting, found at a neighboring garage sale, was proudly displayed in her living room for many years. In her New-Age way of thinking, I am sure this was a type of validation that she was on the right path to enlightenment.

Aunt Willow married young, as did most of her siblings, most likely in order to escape an abusive father and unhealthy home life. She was enamored by her new husband's family, who practiced witchcraft, mysticism and followed the teachings of Edgar Cayce, an American clairvoyant who used self-induced trances to channel spirits for answers on any number of topics. Aunt Willow found that this new form of spirituality could empower her to gain influence, attain what she dreamed about, and possibly help others along the way. Who wouldn't want that? It all seemed relatively harmless, noble, and would even seem to be another way to grow closer to God. On the contrary, and with definite certainty, nothing could be further from the truth. The exact opposite may most likely occur, opening an extremely harmful supernatural door not easily closed.

By today's standards, all of the mysticism, spirit guides, communicating with the dead, and attending spiritualist churches would definitely put you in the socially acceptable, trendy, and popular column on the media page of choice. It is my opinion, however, that this is dangerous ground to tread on and may open some doors that you really don't want to open. My life may have turned out quite differently had I attended my aunt's church and had opened a door or two. Make no mistake, the supernatural is very real, and the devil definitely wants our children. I remain thankful that I can see God's hand of protection throughout my childhood, even though the journey was a rough and often tumultuous one.

Why even bother to add this chapter into my family's history? It is my hope that this information may help to explain why events have unfolded the way they have and why some in my family are more susceptible to the supernatural realm and its effects than others.

Remember my uncle Denny, Aunt Willow's second husband who never made it home from the Vietnam War? As a very little girl, I had the same recurring dream about him that I remember to this very day. I never met the man, in the flesh, on this planet and had only ever seen pictures of him. In the dream, I was visiting a cemetery, and as a very little girl, I have no memory of visiting one that young. While continuing my stroll, I happened upon a plot with black wrought iron fencing surrounding a stone casket perched in its middle, seemingly on a mound. Happily sitting on top of the casket, with a warm and inviting smile, was my uncle Denny. He waved and stated that he had his eye on me. I warmed up to him right away. When the dream ended,

I was always a little sad to be leaving but happy to have had the chance to see him. On a side note, fast forward a few years to the first time I met my husband, Jon, at a college party. His very first words to me ever? "I've got my eye on you." Maybe that's the real reason I married him; he had Uncle Denny's approval.

5

Bloodline Witches

Upon further research, it was discovered that my family lineage included an actual witch, according to my Great-Grandma Jo, who lived in the hills of Virginia. My great-grandmother refused to have anything to do with her mother-in-law, a well-known witch, who actively practiced and pursued witchcraft and the occult due, in part, to an unhappy marriage. Her husband was a mean and evil man who abused her daily. She bound him to his bed by pouring a ring of salt around him as he slept while uttering an incantation. It seemed to have worked. He was bound and stuck in a trance-like state long enough for her to be able to get away from him. Though this may seem hard to believe, I can assure you that witchcraft is as alive and well on planet earth now as it was over eighty years ago.

Wicca and witchcraft were commonplace in the hills of Virginia during the 1930s and 1940s. Survival during the depression was challenging, and those in many areas of rural Virginia could not afford medical attention or medication of any kind. They would seek out natural healers and witches for remedies and aid in removing evil or unwelcomed guests, including their own relatives. There are currently many covens in existence in Virginia and all over the country during the writing of this book, as people continually seek out supernatural answers to their ongoing issues and questions.

It is possible for dysfunctional curses to follow bloodlines and open doors to the supernatural in its descendants for hundreds of years unless broken or interrupted. To have a great-great-grandmother as a self-proclaimed witch, well, let's just say the door's wide open for possible supernatural issues to rear their ugly heads. They did exactly that, many times over in our family.

Aunt Willow may have been pre-disposed to negative supernatural tendencies already since her great-grandmother continually practiced witchcraft. Add to that the fact that Aunt Willow actively desired to become a medium, immersing herself entirely in the New Age culture, and you have a recipe for a supernaturally dysfunctional disaster of epic proportions to occur.

We know that the devil is a master at deception and can disguise himself as an angel or ministering spirit as the Bible states in 2 Corinthians 11:14, "And no wonder, for Satan himself masquerades as an angel of light." He began as the head of the angelic hosts, was beautiful, referred to as a cherub, and believed to have overseen all heavenly music or praise. When talking about the king of Tyre, or Lucifer, God told Ezekiel:

> Son of man, take up a lament concerning the king of Tyre and say to him: "This is what the Sovereign Lord says: 'You were the model of perfection, full of wisdom and perfect in beauty. You were in Eden, the garden of God; every precious stone adorned you: ruby, topaz, and emerald, chrysolite, onyx and jasper, sapphire, turquoise and beryl. Your settings and mountings were made of gold; on the day you were created they were prepared. You were anointed as a guardian cherub, for so I ordained you. You were on the holy mount of God; you walked among the fiery stones.'"
>
> Ezekiel 28:12-14

Lucifer epitomized beauty and perfection according to God, his creator. He, at one time, was blameless and even pure, as difficult as it is for us to imagine. In Latin, his name means "light-bringer," and in Hebrew can be translated as "morning star," "star of the morning," or "bright star." When God describes Lucifer and all the precious beautiful stones in Ezekiel 28:13, He says that the stones and colors were actually in Lucifer, as the Amplified version of the Bible explains it in verse 13, "And the gold, the workmanship of your settings and your sockets, was in you." He emanated gorgeous light that our minds can't even begin to comprehend. Lucifer was a beautiful being in every sense of the word. We know how the story goes; he became too full of himself, puffed up with pride, and desired God's job. But before his fall, his duty was to cover and protect, as God tells us in Ezekiel 28:14, "You were anointed as a guardian cherub, for so I ordained you. You were on the holy mount of God; you walked among the fiery stones."

Lucifer's job included covering and protecting, the total opposite of what he is known for today. He was gorgeous, had it all, and threw it away for his own glory and pleasure. I have to admit; it's challenging for my human brain to understand how he could have left all of that, not to mention the promise of being eternally separated from a loving heavenly Father because of his prideful sin. Knowing a little bit about the devil's backstory may shed some light as to how some people could easily be deceived by the occult or New Age lifestyle, especially since he was such a stunning being in and of himself and can be in disguise as something holy, lovely, or even comforting. Since the devil has his own brigade of fallen angels that do his bidding and can also transform themselves into spirit guides, ghosts, or supposed helpful entities, the possibilities of deception are without end in the New Age or occult culture.

As Paul tells us in 2 Corinthians 11:14-15, "And no wonder, for even Satan himself masquerades as an angel of light. It is not surprising, then, if his servants masquerade as servants of righteousness. Their end will be what their actions deserve."

It's not difficult to understand how those who were struggling in the 1930s and 1940s in the poverty-stricken hills of Virginia may have seen the appeal of using Wicca or witchcraft to alleviate painful symptoms in the body or to escape a life of torment or poverty, especially if deceptive spirits appeared to them or others on their behalf and encouraged their participation with promises of help and hope, which may have been in short supply during that specific point in time.

Dabbling in New Age and occult practices always comes at a high price, the cost of your soul for all eternity. Please believe that though these types of practices may promise prosperity or whatever you ask for under the guise of a comforting spirit guide, psychic, medium, witch, Wiccan, or spiritualist, the devil is the one pulling the strings, always, and he absolutely hates you. You were made in God's image, and you are Satan's arch-nemesis. Though he may appear as a gentle, harmless, sweet spirit, he wants to take you down with him. That is his life's mission, and he's very good at his job. He knows his time is growing short, and he's working overtime to try to kill, steal, and destroy.

I'd like to be able to tell you at this point that those who practice witchcraft or engage and believe in the New Age philosophies will live out their lives without a care in the world, will receive wealth, divine health, and will end up in heaven when their time on this earth is over. I'd truly like to tell you that, but I'd be lying to you. The purpose of this book is to document a series of events that actually happened, back it up with what God tells us in His Word, and allow you to draw your own conclusions.

So, what exactly does God say about witches or mediums, and how does He feel about those who practice divination? In the NIV Bible translation under the heading of "Detestable Practices," Moses was extremely clear about God's feelings on this very matter. In Deuteronomy 18:10-12, the Bible is quoted as stating:

> Let no one be found among you who sacrifices his son or daughter in the fire, who practices divination or sorcery, interprets omens, engages in witchcraft, or casts spells, or who is a medium or spiritist or who consults the dead. Anyone who does these things is detestable to the Lord, and because of these detest-

able practices the Lord your God will drive out those nations before you.

Deuteronomy 18:10-12

The KJV translation of Deuteronomy 18:12 goes so far as to say, "For all that do these things are an abomination unto the Lord." An abomination, according to the dictionary by Merriam-Webster[2], is defined as something that is "regarded with disgust or hatred." The biblical definition of abomination, as mentioned by Wikipedia[3], seems to be a bit harsher. Wikipedia indicates it to be "that which is exceptionally loathsome, hateful, sinful, wicked or vile." Seems perfectly clear to me, God doesn't care for abominations and will not put up with them or their wicked ways.

Moses also mentioned something similar in Leviticus 19:26 (AMP) when God told him, "You shall not eat anything with the blood, nor practice divination [using omens or witchcraft] or soothsaying." It doesn't matter if intentions are for good; any type of practice that God hates or calls an abomination is wrong and rightfully forbidden. He doesn't forbid New Age or occult practices because He's depriving us of anything good or hiding something enlightening from us. We don't know more than our creator and never will, regardless of the lies

2 www.merriam-webster.com
3 www.en.wikipedia.org

the enemy tries to sell us. New Age and occult activities may be detrimental to our minds, bodies, and ultimately, our souls. He's trying to protect us and desires us to spend eternity with Him. John 3:16, "For God so loved the world that he gave his one and only Son, that whoever believes in him shall not perish but have eternal life." It sounds to me like He's on our side and desires that no one spends eternity separated from Him.

I can't speak for my great-great-grandmother, Sarah, the witch who bound her husband and practiced her craft openly, most likely unapologetically, up until the end of her days. But what about my sweet Aunt Willow? Would my loving heavenly Father allow the aunt that I love so much, who is negatively affected by this bloodline curse from her great-grandmother, to spend her afterlife under unending torment and torture in the pit of hell? How could He do that? Well, according to 2 Peter 3:9, "The Lord is not slow about keeping his promise, as some understand slowness. He is patient with you, not wanting anyone to perish, but everyone to come to repentance." Peter reminds us that God wants no one to be lost, and He will patiently wait for us to repent and turn to Him. He's waiting to forgive. All we have to do is ask.

Aunt Willow is now eighty-three years old, still sweet, feisty, and doing well in her little corner of the world. She's alive and kicking on planet Earth, and as long as she is, there is still hope that she will turn to the Lord and have an eternity filled with love and joy. If you were to ask her what she thought of Jesus, our only ticket to heaven, she would tell you, "He's a nice teacher." She's not alone, as many mediums and New Age followers hold the same, unwavering belief. In over forty years of pursuing the Lord, I've finally come to the brilliant realization that it's not my job to judge anyone. You could accurately say that I'm a very slow learner on this point. My job is to love them, lift them up in prayer and let God do His perfect work in them. No one could do it in sheer loving perfection as well as our heavenly Father.

Prayer is a truly powerful tool in dealing with any spirit of the anti-Christ hovering over our loved ones and our country. In the words of Jesus Himself in Matthew 18:18, "I tell you the truth, whatever you bind on earth will be bound in heaven, and whatever you loose on earth will be loosed in heaven." My aunt has a small army of intercessors continually praying on her behalf for salvation, protection, and binding the enemy's strongholds in her life. We won't stop until our prayers are answered. Until then, we will unconditionally love her to the best of our ability into the kingdom of God.

Do bloodline curses truly exist today? Can they be broken? The answers to both questions are emphatically yes, whether we choose to believe it or not. Though it sounds simple enough, and I would agree in theory that it is, the tie must be a desired break for the individual or family it directly affects. You can't sit on the fence with this one; it's all in or all out. I have done this with my family, ending any hold the curse has tried to put on any of us. Though I must admit, not before the supernaturally dysfunctional genes reared their ugly unwanted heads with scary and devastating results.

6

Legion

My mother had five sisters and three brothers who all lived nearby, except for a brother who lived across the country. I had the luxury of growing up with aunts, uncles, and cousins all around me for impromptu cookouts and every major or minor holiday. If any of the parents went away for a trip or weekend, we stayed with family. Needless to say, the cousins were always thrown in the mix, and we found ways to entertain each other with games or some kind of mischief, as kids often do. I love all my crazy cousins and am very grateful that they were a major part of my childhood and life.

One holiday stands out as it drastically changed our lives and outlook on the reality of unwelcomed supernatural influences. After dinner, I was hanging out with my cousin, Babs. She began to nervously tell me about things that had been happening to her when no one else was around. She mentioned that she would begin scratching herself uncontrollably and even showed me the proof on her arm. She told me there were times when she felt as though she was being choked or that her chest was being compressed, making it difficult to breathe. Being the self-absorbed teenager that I was at the time, I did manage to listen to her but then quickly dismissed the story and most likely went out to get more dessert, forgetting what I had just been told. You see, Babs has had a learning disability since birth and is seven years older than I am. She has always been a little slow but still a sweet soul, at least to me. I spent countless nights staying at her home throughout my entire childhood, as cousins often did back then.

Several days after that holiday gathering, my mother and I were casually talking when something prompted me to tell her the story that Babs had unfolded in confidence after dinner. I admit that I almost didn't say anything at all because I didn't deem it as newsworthy. Thank goodness God got me to open my mouth and spill the beans. I remember the look on Mom's face, eyes widening and color slightly draining, as I explained the full story in great detail. I guess I listened a little better than I thought at the time. She never said a word, even when I finished talking, so again the topic was forgotten, at least as far as I knew.

Since my mom was and still is very close to Babs's mother, Aunt Ellie, she wasted no time in getting together with her to discuss what Mom had heard from me and had witnessed herself on that same holiday gathering. I found out much later that my mom had noticed how Babs would never look her directly in the eyes and that when she did lock eyes with Mom, Bab's eyes had changed. Babs would stare at my mother with hatred, and we now know evil, but the strangest part was the actual physical changes she noticed in them. She said that Babs's eyes would glaze over at times, as she had seen before in my grandmother, who suffered from Alzheimer's. Her eyes would also seem to change color and darken, which was more than a little unsettling to my mother.

As the conversation continued, Aunt Ellie went on to tell my mom about things she had been noticing lately with her daughter. Babs was exhibiting ongoing strange behavior and was often extremely angry, unruly, or mean-spirited. She had injured Aunt Ellie on several occasions. Both my aunt and uncle were unable to physically ward off her outbursts or attacks that continually grew worse with each passing day.

Mom and Aunt Ellie decided to take Babs to LeSea's Christian Center Church office in Indiana. They met with a minister who specialized in such cases in the hopes of receiving counseling or at least uncover a way to help Babs with whatever she was going through. The events that followed their initial meeting started a domino effect in the lives of my aunt and her family, with lingering ripples of shockwaves that to this day still haunt my mother while leaving its proverbial gash in our ancestral family tree.

It wasn't very far into the meeting and not long after polite introductions were made before evil manifested right before their eyes in the guise of my cousin, Babs. As the minister placed his hand on Babs's head and began praying, a deep male voice spewed vile words out of her mouth while her face contorted and changed before their very eyes. She then began writhing and twisting on the floor while hissing as if she were a serpent while everyone in the room continued to pray. With great spiritual authoritative force, the minister then commanded the demon to leave Babs. It screamed and continued speaking in a deep, guttural male voice, using intelligent verbiage that one who couldn't even write her own name would never have known. That's when it was discovered that there was more than one demon cohabitating within her, just as the title at the beginning of this chapter stated from Mark 5:9, "'My name is Legion,' he replied, 'for we are many.'"

Unfortunately, this event continued to reveal itself while closely resembling some of the exorcism movies that are being shown today. The hideous voice began weaving its story of having a hold on her by keeping her in a child-like state through cartoon television programs aired during that time. It actually mentioned the exact names of well-known, popular cartoon shows of the day. It was also quoted as saying, "We got her from those lusty, filthy soap operas." Through screaming, swearing, and intelligent sentences in a voice resembling one straight out of a nightmarish horror movie, the entities did everything possible to try to distract the prayers and commands from the minister who demanded they leave my cousin permanently. After, what I can only imagine being hours of combative spiritual warfare, he was able to free Babs from the demonic grip that had tormented her for years, using the name of Jesus. Demons tremble at the name of Jesus and must obey when believers use it properly. Philippians 2:9, "Therefore God exalted him to the highest place and gave him the name that is above every name."

My Catholic friends may be wondering how a mere minister could have exorcised a demonic spirit from my cousin since he was not Catholic and obviously no priest. After all, the movies portray that only priests are able to do such supernaturally unsettling and horrifying exorcisms. Well, the Bible is clear on that point, as Jesus Himself explained:

> I tell you the truth, anyone who has faith in me will do what I have been doing. He will do even greater things than these, because I am going to the Father. And I will do whatever you ask in my name, so that the Son may

bring glory to the Father. You may ask me for
anything in my name, and I will do it.

John 14:12-14

Jesus explained to us that whoever believes in Him
will have the authority to do what He has done and do
even greater things, including driving demons out of
tormented individuals. In Mark chapter 6, Jesus instructed His twelve disciples to go, teach the people and
drive out evil spirits. Mark went on to tell us in Mark
6:13, "They drove out many demons and anointed many
sick people with oil and healed them." Mark mentioned
that they, as believers, drove out demons with the authority of the name of Jesus. We have the authority to
do the same, though I'm not suggesting you head out in
search of exorcisms to perform unless God has prompted you to do so.

It also should be stated that the minister my family
met with was a direct descendant of the incomparable
Lester Sumrall, who was known for evangelizing all
over the world, casting out demons, and doing miraculous healings all in the name of Jesus. This minister undoubtedly knew what he was doing and learned, hands
down, from the very best in the business.

Though Babs was delivered that day from her demonic possession, she wasn't entirely free for quite
some time. When demons are exorcised and driven out,

especially when there are many, they are known to go out and recruit several more and try to return to their freshly cleaned out home to continue their torment:

> When an evil spirit comes out of a man, it goes through arid places seeking rest and does not find it. Then it says, "I will return to the house I left." When it arrives, it finds the house unoccupied, swept clean and put in order. Then it goes and takes with it seven other spirits more wicked than itself, and they go in and live there. And the final condition of the man is worse than the first.
>
> Matthew 12:43-45

The battle wasn't completely over for Babs or my aunt and uncle. They spent countless hours praying over Babs and continually saturated her with Scripture, officially ending the devil's hold on her once and for all. Today, I am happy to report she is totally free from the demons that had been her source of pain and torment for many years.

Since, at this point in time, the entire family was aware of the fact that Aunt Willow was a practicing medium, guess who was blamed for my cousin's demonic possession issues? Exactly. My aunt Willow endured the brunt of the blame from well-meaning family members who believed her occult practices must have ushered in the unwelcomed spirits and caused such terror and pain. As a teenager, I wrote to my aunt about it, as email had not yet existed, and I wasn't allowed to read her response. She was basically shunned from my life for a while, and no one in the family had much to do with her, which may not seem like a very Christianly thing to do. Looking back, I know that witnessing such a horrific scene straight out of an exorcism movie had lasting effects on my mom and Aunt Ellie. They were going to do everything possible to prevent it from happening again to anyone else. They understandably felt that Aunt Willow was somehow channeling the demonic, thus obviously causing all the issues. They may have been partly right, but not entirely. This devilish foothold had been established years ago through our own ancestral bloodline curses. Things are rarely as they seem. The unseen supernatural forces that are continually hovering around us insert their presence whenever possible. Their intention would be to wreak havoc, destroy lives and continually cause unrelenting severe dysfunction. At this point, however, the family breathed a heavy sigh of relief, as evil had obviously left the building. Or had it?

7

Sins of the Father

Flash-forward several years in the life of my aunt Ellie and her family; Babs has a younger brother, Bradley, who was married with two beautiful children. His kids grew up hanging around their grandparent's house and, for a while, lived right next door to my aunt and uncle's home. The family was always together and loved to go camping. In fact, it seemed as if that's what they did most weekends during the summer months. Aunt Ellie, the doting grandmother, babysat as often as she could and loved spending time with them all.

A few years into his marriage, his once overweight wife lost around thirty or forty pounds, engaged in an affair, had breast enhancement surgery, and promptly left her family. My aunt and uncle helped Bradley out with the kids as much as they could, especially during such a difficult time. My cousin, one of the sweetest guys on the planet, was the best dad with the biggest heart of gold. He did not deserve all that he had to deal with. He lovingly raised and provided for his family without complaint and with unwavering faith. He loves the Lord and loves his family.

Years of raising his children without their mother were challenging ones for Bradley. As the kids got older, it was learned that his son was bipolar and needed to continually be on medication to avoid behavioral problems. The meds seemed to work for Cass, now a teenager, as long as he consistently remembered to take them. It was also around this time that Cass's mother, and Bradley's ex-wife, Janet, began to come around to stir up trouble as often as she could, which didn't help the stress factor for their entire family. She wanted money and began to get close to her children to use them somehow for her own financial gain. Janet grew especially close to her daughter, Brinn. Brinn, now a beautiful teenager, began spending more and more time with her mother.

Seemingly out of nowhere and extremely unexpectedly, the accusations against my uncle flooded the family, now shocked, bewildered, and in utter disbelief. Brinn, along with her mother, approached Bradley and told him that her grandfather had been molesting her for as long as she could remember. Horrified and heartbroken, Bradley confronted my uncle in the presence of Aunt Ellie. I'm sure my aunt most likely was thinking this to be another disgusting plan for Brinn's mother to get money from the family until my uncle opened his mouth. He stated that whatever Brinn had said was true. I'm sure it took all the strength that Bradley had to restrain himself from punching his father or beating him senselessly right then and there. To this day, I don't know how he held it together. They immediately brought charges up against my uncle, who went to jail and ultimately prison, as my aunt's world began to unravel.

It was on that very day that Aunt Ellie, the sweetest, most gentle, generous, and loving Christian woman on the face of the planet, had lost all hope. She had been with this man since her teenage years growing up in Virginia yet had no idea of the demented evil that lurked in his soul. How could she have been so blind? I'm sure she blamed herself for being unable to protect Brinn. Aunt Ellie saw no signs of her husband's wicked tendencies whatsoever. As she thought back to all the camping trips and times that her husband was alone with their granddaughter, her heart ached, her stomach tightened, she felt dizzy, lost her breath, and lost her will to live.

I believe it was later that day when I received a phone call from my aunt Gracie, the youngest sister of my mom and Aunt Ellie. My aunt wanted to let me know that Aunt Ellie had tried to kill herself and that my mother was with her at the hospital. Aunt Gracie unfolded the entire incident to me, a young mom at the time. As I sat there in a state of shock, I'm ashamed to admit that my first questions to my aunt were along the lines of wondering if my uncle was going to get any help as he was obviously sick. What! To this day, I have no idea why I would have even thought that way at all. This man chose to do evil instead of getting help. He destroyed lives. My sweet, precious aunt was in the emergency room after trying to kill herself; as a Christian, knowing full well that her death would ultimately mean an eternity apart from Jesus, all because of an evil, selfish, and unrepentant man. Aunt Ellie felt responsible and hopeless and an all-consuming sorrow over what had happened to her granddaughter that she loved so much and couldn't protect. My aunt wasn't asking or crying out for help when she slit her own wrists. She was done with her life. She had already dealt with a demonically possessed child, had overcome that with God's help, and this was her reward? Finding out that her husband, believed to have been her best friend for all those years, was, in fact, an incestuous pedophile. It was just more than she could bear.

How could a loving God allow this to happen to her? To her family? I asked my aunt Gracie those very questions, and I'll never forget her patient response. She told me that this was meant to come to light so that my uncle could be criminally charged and prosecuted for what he had done. God made it clear and had allowed it to be uncovered in order that no one else could be hurt by him.

Aunt Gracie enlightened me with a couple of stories of her own personal run-ins with my uncle, having been very young herself when Aunt Ellie was married. She said he always made her uncomfortable and had grabbed and brushed up against her many times. She had learned to keep her distance from him. I'm so glad she did.

I must admit that I also took some comfort in knowing how fellow incarcerated inmates often treated pedophiles while in prison and prayed accordingly. Yes, I lost my religion a little bit when it came to this disgraceful person that I used to call my uncle. How do you forgive someone like him? People may often say we are to "hate the sin, but not the sinner." I have to be honest in stating that in some cases, this is extremely difficult to do. Unfortunately for me and my family, God is very clear on this point as well: Matthew 6:15, "But if you do not forgive men their sins, your Father will not forgive your sins." It's emphasized in red in my Bible, folks. The exact words from the mouth of Jesus. According to the Bible, God loves my ex-uncle just as much as He loves me, and I have no right whatsoever to hate him. I must forgive, or else I can't be forgiven. Clear, simplistic, true, and painful. If I had a hard time forgiving this evil man, I can't even begin to imagine how painfully and practically impossible it would have been for my cousin, Bradley, or Aunt Ellie to forgive him. Your father and husband should be the protector, supporter, and leader of the family, not evil incarnate. Though I can't speak for how they healed and were able to move on with their lives, I do believe that with God, "all things are possible," as Jesus stated in Matthew 19:26. He knows that we are human and would be challenged at times, especially with unforgiveness, since He was God on earth in human form Himself. He knows us inside and out, as well as all our flaws and continual tendencies to let Him down. But He also tells us that His mercies are new every morning. In all honestly, this entire family needs His merciful love, peace, and comfort every single day, especially during this gut-wrenching, unfathomable, and insane time in our history. In Lamentations 3:22-23, it is recorded that "Because of the Lord's great love we are consumed, for his compassions never fail. They are new every morning." I remain humbly and extremely grateful for that.

As I was on the phone with Aunt Gracie, trying to wrap my brain around all that had happened, my mother sat by Aunt Ellie's side in the hospital, covering her with prayer. Aunt Ellie began to wake up and started sharing with her sister. One of the very first things my aunt, who had just almost died, asked my mom was about me. I had stayed over at my aunt's house more

times than I could count as a child, and she was worried
that my uncle had also molested me. She asked about
my aunt Gracie's daughters as well. Mom assured her
that he hadn't had the chance to hurt anyone else and
tried to comfort Aunt Ellie to the best of her ability.
My aunt had undoubtedly been through hell on earth,
many times over, and was selflessly worrying about everyone else. That is the gentle nature of Aunt Ellie, in a
nutshell.

I believe it is safe to say that my aunt was angry at
God for quite a while. Her physical healing was relatively quick, but her emotional and spiritual healing took
a bit longer. She began to realize that her husband had
also, most likely, molested their own daughter, Babs, for
years on end. In fact, it was obviously conclusive that he
was the overwhelming reason Babs had suffered from
demonic possession in the first place and that it was not
the fault of my aunt Willow, the self-proclaimed family
medium, who had been previously blamed for it.

The major dysfunction in this family was supernaturally charged by open doors that spanned several generations and had ultimately enjoyed a long, free reign
over them. Generational curses are believed to be inherited from our parents as the result of descendants in the
ancestral bloodline that in some way opened the door
to the enemy through sin. This then allowed the devil
a stronghold or claim to members of that particular

family line until the curse could be broken. The problem is that many don't know of its existence until evil begins to manifest itself and the devil tips his hand, so to speak. In certain circles, it is believed that 99 percent of curses, torments, diseases, and broken families are due to sins, abominations, cursed things, or blaspheming God. Since the door to curses may have been opened by any one of those things, the devil seeks to destroy all by blinding the eyes of the tormented so that they are unable to see the doors that have been opened to him. Another one of his favorite things to do is to get family members to blame each other for all the negative things or major problems that happen in their lives. I'm sad to say that this plan worked very well in our family for a while.

It was also uncovered through my studies that the curse of suicide is one of several that our ancestors are plagued with. Aunt Ellie had an uncle who succeeded in committing suicide. It was noted that depression and suicidal thoughts were very prevalent in several family members throughout our history, and several to this day still battle depression at varying degrees.

Aunt Ellie recovered and divorced her husband, as he was sent to prison. She remains close to her son, Bradley, but is estranged from her grandchildren, who want nothing more to do with her because of their grandfather's actions. Aunt Ellie paid the price, and then some, for his wicked behavior. Despite all she had to endure, she has made her peace with the Lord and is doing very well to this day. I believe she still takes time to read and study God's Word. She believes in His promises and that His words are true. She is not bitter but rather gentle, loving, sweet-spirited, strong-willed, and full of God's grace. By today's standards, she would have every right in the world to remain angry or hold grudges, but she chooses to love. That is a miracle. She is a true miracle.

8

Broken and Abused

I am thankful to be a part of a legacy of strong men and women who drew lines in their ancestral sand and stopped the devil in his tracks. My mother, my aunts, and uncles all had excuses to be hate-filled and abusive, but they chose love instead. The household they grew up in was the exact opposite of love.

This has been the most challenging chapter to write about in my family's history. I have purposefully stepped away from the keyboard for a week of soul-searching and prayer that I might be able to describe events in a factual and effective way. The supernatural attacks that have ensued during my time away from you have ensured the importance of the topic. As uncomfortable as it is to write about, it's time. I have a feeling that many families across our country can relate in some way to the events that transpired in my family line or at least know of many who have suffered or witnessed life-threatening abuse in varying degrees.

Grandma Mimi was married at a very young age to a prominent, well-respected man in a small Virginian community. Between them, she and Dicky Lee had nine children who survived as well as one set of twins that were stillborn.

Dicky Lee put on his very best face and attire when he was out in public. They, in turn, thought him a prince among men. He was known to help other families and children in need and even preached at the local Baptist church when the presiding pastor was away. There is no way on earth that anyone in the community would have said a harsh word against this wonderful man, who was from a highly esteemed family, appeared to do so much for so many, and who obviously had a loving, happy family at home who were lucky to have such a man to take care of them. If we have learned anything from my family history so far, it would be the fact that nothing is ever as it seems and that evil can be well-hidden in practically perfect people. No, he was nothing like Mary Poppins.

If I had to break down some interesting discoveries learned from interviewing family members concerning their father's personality traits, it would be safe to say that Dicky Lee was an evil, consistently abusive, and narcissistic man. And yes, believe it or not, those are his good points!

I can appreciate the definition from www.dictionary.com, which stated a narcissist to be "a person who is overly self-involved, and often vain and selfish." A narcissist often lacks empathy, has feelings of entitlement, and may continually seek validation or approval of his magnified view of himself as a human being by others, whose opinions he highly valued. He could also become severely impatient or angry when neglecting to receive the special treatment he daily demanded and so desperately desired to feel important. He would often belittle others to make himself feel superior, as was often witnessed in his very own household.

It is safe to assume that Dicky Lee was most likely the product of an abusive environment himself while growing up. As several well-known television Bible teachers have been heard on many occasions to simply yet accurately state, "Hurting people hurt people." Having taken a few psychology courses in my day, I can wholeheartedly agree with that statement. Understanding why individuals succumb to their abusive tendencies still does not excuse their unspeakable behavior. It would also seem evident that Dicky Lee's abusive rampages undoubtedly stemmed from some type of supernatural bloodline curse since he must have grown up in a similarly overtly dysfunctional and brutal type of atmosphere. He took it up a notch to another level, which is hard to envision, knowing the gentle and loving disposition of his offspring as I do.

In his household, Dicky Lee's wants and needs always came first. He had high-quality food that only he was allowed to eat, while his family had scraps or went without. He had nice clothes, while his children did not. Yes, my grandmother sewed, made their clothes from scraps of cloth she could get and taught her daughters how to sew as well. But Dickie Lee did very little to help support his growing family. Though he always managed to have enough money to help other children or families, in order that he looked honorable and noble. In the eyes of the community, his generosity knew no bounds. Add to that the fact that he also had enough money to drink himself into a stupor at the local bar many nights on a weekly basis. It is believed that he may have also done a little bootlegging on the side and loved the local ladies who frequented those hangouts as well. A true gentleman. A man's man. Until he decided to go home. It was then that this guest preacher for the local Baptist church and well-respected man about town let the mask slip and would allow his true colors to emerge. After all, it takes a lot of energy to keep the façade of God's gift to Grundy up all day long.

My grandmother and her children walked on eggshells around Dicky Lee. They did their best to be quiet when he was home, to stay out of his way, and to be careful to answer him in a manner so as not to provoke his anger that could erupt at a moment's notice. He repeatedly and almost daily beat and raped my grandmother, which is undoubtedly why she birthed eleven children. She did her best to protect them, but they often incurred the brunt of his undeserved wrath as well. He beat them often for as long as they could remember and even stomped on them when they were defenseless babies. I cannot comprehend such a horrific evil that would stomp on helpless babies or hurt little children. It is truly a miracle that they survived living with Dickie Lee at all.

On one afternoon, something set Dickie Lee off, and he began to beat my grandmother until she lay bloodied on the floor. While he was bent over her, in nothing but his underwear, still hitting her and banging her head on the floor, his young daughters ran out of the room to find their older brother in the hopes of getting help. They were all afraid that Dickie Lee was going to kill their mother. My uncle Frankie, then a teenager, grabbed his new hunting rifle, ran into the living room, and pointed it at Dickie Lee's head, demanding that he get away from his mother. Dicky Lee stood up, slowly inching toward my young uncle while saying something along the lines of, "Now Frankie, you aren't going to shoot me." Uncle Frankie cocked his gun, looked him directly in the eye, and answered, "If you don't get out of this house right now, I surely will." Dicky Lee left, dignity in-tact, wearing only his tidy whiteys. I believe he was jailed shortly after for drunkenness along with indecent exposure. The pride of the community's true colors shone brightly that day for all to see.

At this point in time, my grandmother knew that when her husband got out of jail, he would undoubtedly come back and most likely finish what he had started. His anger would be greatly escalated to the point where he could quite possibly kill them all. She knew she had a small window of time to get everyone out of the house before he would be released from jail. Aunt Ellie was newly married and had moved to Indiana, where her new husband had found a good job. After my grandmother had contacted them, Aunt Ellie and her husband rushed to Virginia to rescue them all and take them back to Indiana, where they began their new life. Soon after, Grandma Mimi divorced Dicky Lee. My mother, Lucy Anne, was only nine years old at the time.

Undoubtedly, Dickie Lee was pre-disposed to abusing his family due to the behavior he witnessed or the abuse he himself had suffered during his childhood. His environment was probably one that de-valued women, thought children a burden, and believed loose morals permittable without consequence for the husband or head of the household. Imagine my best impersonation of SNL's Church Lady's character as she might explain who was truly behind Dickie Lee's narcissistic, hateful, and extremely abusive behavior, "Oh, I don't know, could it be...Satan?" I would like to think that, had the Church Lady met Dicky Lee, she would have blatantly declared that very statement to which I would wholeheartedly agree. The puppeteer behind such supernatural dysfunctionality most definitely would be the enemy and his minions. A little bit of the devil, a lot of free will, and an unwillingness to change or try to be a decent human being that loves, nurtures, and protects their family instead of continually beating them practically to death sums up a miserable soul that assuredly died alone in his unrepentant sin.

Abuse of any kind belongs in the category of bloodline curses and supernatural dysfunctionality. Since Dickie Lee was most likely abused, he grew up and, in turn, abused his wife and children. Though this tendency to abuse makes sense to us and explains his behavior, it in no way excuses it. As a grown man with known anger issues, he could have learned self-control, gone to counseling, therapy, or the church pastor, and could have found ways to overcome those terrible tendencies instead of embracing them or fueling the fire with alcohol.

I admit that knowing Dickie Lee's history, I would be extremely curious to know what he actually preached about at that Baptist church in Virginia when his own pastor was away. Knowing he was a hateful, abusive drunk, who womanized, never provided well for his family, and beat his wife and children almost to death, I find it challenging to imagine him preaching in a manner that made any type of sense at all. I wonder about the topics chosen for his hypocritical sermons and if he ever mentioned Jesus or his love? I do know that because of his filling in for the pastor, while all along being the devil incarnate at home, my mother had a very hard time with religion or believing in God for many years following their move away from her evil biological father. Dickie Lee was the reason it took her so long to find her faith in the Lord. In the words of Jesus Himself, He declared in Matthew 18:6, "But if anyone causes one of these little ones who believe in me to sin, it would be better for him to have a large millstone hung around his neck and to be drowned in the depths of the sea." It sounds to me as if the Lord takes such things extremely seriously, as Dickie Lee may have already found out, up close and personally upon his untimely demise.

It is important at this point to emphasize that not one of Dickie Lee's children went on to abuse or beat their own spouses or children in any way, shape, or form. All nine of his children broke the abusive bloodline curse, ending the supernaturally dysfunctional tendencies that most assuredly tried to manifest themselves throughout their individual lifetimes. My aunts and uncles were loving, generous, and well-adjusted adults who nurtured and supported their families as well as each other when difficulties arose. They were abused themselves from their time of birth as well as throughout their entire childhoods. They would have had every excuse, by society's standards, to lean towards abusing their own families but rather chose not to follow in their father's footsteps. They chose love, charity, and a future full of promise instead of extreme discontentment, anger, and hate. It is my personal belief that anyone can control their own behavior and change if their desire is strong enough, especially with the help of the Lord. My family broke the abusive stronghold the enemy tried to impart on them before any of them even had a personal relationship with Jesus, which is an amazing miracle. So, if mere mortals who didn't even have the God-given authority and power yet granted to them because of Jesus' death on the cross, who hadn't at that time accepted His sacrifice and salvation, could control their anger and refrain from beating their own children, after suffering years of abuse and torment themselves, then no one on this planet has any excuse for such vile, abhorrently evil, and contemptible behavior.

Paul mentions in Ephesians 6:4:

> Fathers, do not provoke your children to anger [do not exasperate them to the point of

resentment with demands that are trivial or unreasonable or humiliating or abusive; nor by showing favoritism or indifference to any of them], but bring them up [tenderly, with lovingkindness] in the discipline and instruction of the Lord.

Ephesians 6:4 (AMP)

I love the way the Amplified version explains in detail exactly what the Lord demands of all fathers through Paul's writings. It is extremely clear to me that parents are to bring their children up tenderly with love and without abuse or humiliation of any kind. That is God's desire for every household all over the world. God, Himself, is the best example of an unconditionally loving father. My biological grandfather failed his family miserably.

Paul mentions something similar:

Fathers, do not provoke or irritate or exasperate your children [with demands that are trivial or unreasonable or humiliating or abusive; nor by favoritism or indifference; treat them tenderly with lovingkindness], so they will not lose heart and become discouraged or unmotivated [with their spirits broken].

Colossians 3:21 (AMP)

Continual abusive behavior administered on a daily basis from a parent whose main purpose should have been to love and protect would undoubtedly break any child's spirit while embedding deep psychological and emotional scars as well.

At the time of Dickie Lee's severely abusive behavior, none in his household followed the religion of the day, the one that he so hypocritically professed publicly in the pulpit from time to time. He was undeniably a poor example of Christ's love for us. But God intervened. God had other plans for my grandmother and her children. I am sure that he looked on in disdain through all their sorrow as well as their continual mental and physical torment. He must have heard the silent cries of the hearts of those who were broken and abused. As the Scripture tells us in Psalm 22:24, "For he has not despised or disdained the suffering of the afflicted one; he has not hidden his face from him but has listened to his cry for help." He heard the silent cries in the innumerable tears of the abused in that household. He was aware of every single tear that fell, as a cry or prayer for help. He had a divine plan of escape for my grandmother, mother, aunts, and uncles. Because of his gracious love and tender mercy, I am here today with a family of my own.

9

Angelic Glimpses and Holy Rollers

I grew up a Methodist, while my husband, Jon, was raised in the Catholic church. As you could imagine, I had a lot of questions for him about his faith when we first got married and started our family. I could never understand why they prayed to Mary, the mother of Jesus, or to any of the saints. How did that work? Did they really believe in receiving answered prayer from any of their saints? I mean, didn't they have a direct line to God through Jesus, as all Methodists do? My husband has always been a sweet, extremely patient, and highly intelligent man. I found it fascinating that he could never give me a straight answer to the questions I asked him. He simply replied that they "just do." According to my hubby, Catholic parishioners would say different types of prayers to saints for any number of issues simply out of tradition. It took quite a long while for us to find a church in the middle, one that was neither Catholic nor

Methodist and one that we could both agree on. I could compare our church-finding journey to that of avid garage sale shopping fanatics. You want to find the best deal, hidden treasures, and a nice safe sanitary atmosphere with complete anonymity. Upon stopping by a garage sale or local church that seemed a bit dirty, unruly, or uncomfortable, we developed the lost art of bolting at warped speed with ninja precision so as not to be noticed. Still, we weekly shopped for a church with our scavenger hunt-type list of items we deemed important for it to be a worthy choice or good fit for our young and growing family.

Until we were led to a Baptist church in a small city surrounding the Louisville, Kentucky area, we had never attended a Baptist gathering and had no idea of what their Sunday services would look like. Jon and I were both accustomed to a service where we would sing songs from a hymnal, hear Scripture read, partake in an offering, and hear a sermon given before the benediction. Straightforward, simplistic, and steeped in tradition. We would usually sit towards the back of a church during the service for the quickest escape without having to shake a hand or meet the pastor. One Sunday in particular, we sat smack dab in the middlemost part of the center section in the relatively good-sized sanctuary area. We had direct eye contact with the pastor. Let the games begin.

The pastoral church greetings ensued as the service started. There was nothing out of the ordinary so far. Quick announcements were made, and the music started. It seemed a bit early for that but okay. Clearly, the Baptists have their own way of doing things, and we could appreciate that. The music seemed to be a cross between the contemporary Christian genre and a little bit of that southern gospel, old-time religion. Slightly more of a country twang than our rock and roll roots preferred, but we were then living in the Kentucky area, and it was to be expected. The music amped up at that point, and suddenly, it happened. People got out of their pews and began jumping up and down, dancing down the aisles, raising and often almost flapping or flailing their arms as if at any moment they could take off in flight across the sanctuary. All we could do was watch them in disbelief. I'm sure we looked a little confused and totally out of our element as the songs continued for what seemed like forever instead of minutes. I know my thoughts turned to my poor, sweet, traditionally Catholic husband, who I was sure had never witnessed such a spectacle in a real live church. Though uncomfortably aware of my surroundings, I had previously attended several non-Methodist, Christian services growing up, where attendees would dance, clap, and let the spirit move them however they wanted. I didn't care for the sight at that point in time but somewhat understood what was unfolding before our eyes. As the music slowed, so did their dance moves. Worship continued, arms were still raised, and most of the congregation swayed as if in a trance-like state of being. I breathed a sigh of relief as everyone settled in for what would obviously seem to be prayer time. The music continued to lightly play in the background as all singing ceased for what seemed to be a minute or so. An associate pastor went on stage and began to pray. He raised his hands and then began to chant in incoherent sounds of what I'm sure my husband thought to be babbling. Not only did he continue to pray in an unknown tongue, but the entire congregation followed in suit and did the same. As soon as the chanting began in one individual, another from across the room would announce their own interpretation of what the Lord was apparently saying to his flock. I felt the heat begin to travel up my legs until it finally found its resting place on the top of my head, now also tingling with fear. All I could do was silently pray, "Oh dear Lord, please don't let Jon bolt down the aisle and leave me alone to fend for myself." I remember being almost afraid to look at my husband when prayer time finally ended and was surprised that when I opened my eyes, he was still actually sitting beside me—what a trooper. I'm sure the pastor's Sunday message was very nice, though I remain equally sure neither one of us was able to focus on his words.

Our world had officially been rocked on that fate-
ful day. Not only that, but we had remained trapped
throughout the entire service, in the middle pew, directly within the pastor's eye line. Our usual back of the
church positioning in case of emergency or supernatural manifestation antics had failed us miserably, as we
strategically placed ourselves where even the world's
greatest ninja himself would have been unable to leave,
sight unseen. Needless to say, we never returned to that
particular Baptist church, as we seemed to have been
an inappropriate fit at that time in our lives. After our
unexpected experience, the next church of choice would
be Jon's preference, hands down, as I'm pretty sure the
Baptist church had been my idea to visit.

Today we can thoughtfully joke about our first holy-
rolling experience. We were in our early to mid-twen-
ties and were relatively new parents. Our boys were one
and three at the time. We didn't know much but were
sure that we needed to find a good church home to attend as a family. One that would fit all our criteria and
checked off all the boxes on our religiosity list. That
church wasn't our ideal then, but it opened the door to
many future discussions. I'm very thankful for its lesson. Always stick to the escape plan, never stray from
the proven formula, and never-ever sit in the direct eye
line of the pastor!

By the way, fast forward twenty-eight years and take a guess as to where my husband always makes sure to sit while attending church? In the first few rows of the sanctuary, as close to the pastor as possible and always in his direct line of sight. We purposefully stay in the hot seat, at every church or Christian event that we attend, in the hopes of absorbing God's message like the sponges we are.

Yet another baby, a couple of states and five moves later, our family wound up owning a home in Waynesboro, Virginia. We found a cute little Assemblies of God Church that we frequented and came to know many in the congregation. The pastor was young, charismatic, and seemed to have good, biblically foundational messages each week. My husband was enriched and encouraged, which ultimately lead to his acceptance of Jesus and his genuine salvation. He was forever changed, a priceless by-product of finally finding a church we could all call home. We immersed ourselves into the church culture, attended all functions, took classes, and I even taught a Sunday school class.

As our faith began to grow, and as we made a few friends in our new church family, we desired to attend Bible studies or try to start programs to deepen our knowledge of the Lord, as well as to find ways to help the church grow or enrich the lives of others. We were hungry for all that God wanted for us and desired to be used for His purposes, to bring Him glory. At least, that's where our hearts were at the time. Hungry, searching, and wanting the presence of the Lord to guide us to do His perfect will and to be a blessing to Him, as well as those around us.

One Sunday after church, I approached the pastor and his wife and asked if it would be possible for them, or more specifically her, to start a women's Bible study, as a few of the ladies had expressed an interest in attending one on a weekly basis. I remember the pastor never really made eye contact with me and mumbled something about not having the time and that he would need to give it some thought. His answer seemed a little odd to me, so I offered to start one myself to take any pressure off him or his wife. He stated that he didn't think it a good idea and questioned my intentions since I needed to be sure I was wanting to lead the study with a pure heart instead of a self-promoting one. I was crushed. I did then ask him that as my pastor, couldn't he discern the true intentions of my heart and know that it had nothing to do with selfish gain? At that point, I was simply dismissed, the matter dropped, at least as far as he was concerned. I just couldn't let it go. The entire encounter left a bad taste in my mouth, and as my stubborn, dysfunctional supernatural bloodline would demand, I decided to do something about it.

My dear friend, Beth, helped me to study and prepare for our first women's Bible study that would meet at my home. We invited a few of the women from our church who had also shown an interest in an ongoing study, and voila! The revolution had begun! We gathered several times, enjoyed prayer, fellowship, and encouraged each other in the Word. What could be better? The more appropriate question should have been, "What could go wrong?"

It wasn't long before the assumed overtly busy and uninterested wife of the pastor decided to attend our growing home Bible study as well. We had nothing to hide and welcomed her with open arms. We were excited that she could finally experience our Bible study and see all the support and positive engagement in subject matter along with the way we blessed each other.

As the evening progressed, I noticed an uncomfortable feeling in the room. The ladies were guarded and reluctant to participate in any type of discussion concerning the study. I found myself looking forward to the end of the evening and release of whatever spirit that seemed to have overtaken our small, once animated, and outgoing group.

Then came time for prayer. There was only one prayer request made that night. The pastor's wife asked that we all lay hands on her and pray, as she had been going through some terrible issues. We all did as she asked and immediately gathered around, laying hands on her as tears ran down her cheeks and she began to wail. Not a silent cry, she wailed. Her hands raised; she was still moaning and crying as we prayed for whatever she was going through and asked God to intervene and free her of whatever was happening in her life. She commanded attention, took over the evening, and thus forever ended the first women's Bible study we had created for the women in the church.

She had been sent, by her pastoral husband, to see what was happening in the group and put an end to it once and for all. He wanted control of everyone and everything that happened in the church. He got what he wanted, as the ladies presumably were told not to come back to the study since we were doing everything improperly.

In hindsight, I'm surprised that I didn't think about the fact that he had no control over who I could invite into my home or how we decided to read or study God's Word. Not only was he demanding that we were not permitted to hold Bible studies outside of the church without his knowledge, but he also branded my friend and me as the proverbial pot stirrers of the church. I remember wondering how a spirit-filled pastor could not discern my intentions or why he didn't just start a Bible study, to begin with, when everyone was asking for one? Perhaps the pastor, himself, lacked the spirit of discernment, as he was relatively young and appeared to be lacking in other pastoral graces as well. I'm extremely surprised that I didn't go toe-to-toe with him or get directly in his face to at least tell him exactly what I thought of his cowardly actions, as those in my family line are prone to do. Pastor or not, I remain satisfied in the presumption that I would have, undoubtedly, not stopped until I, at the least, had made him cry. Did I mention that God still had His hands full with me in my younger days, and I undoubtedly had much to learn? Believe me; I've spent lots of time on His potter's wheel and sometimes wonder if I'll ever get off it.

Even though I had been hurt by the pastor and his wife's actions, I didn't want to take my husband away from the church where he received his salvation. The pastor was very good at getting people saved and delivering the message of salvation; I'm just not so sure he knew what to do with them once they were saved.

Through prayer, soul-searching, and working on that forgiveness thing, we stayed at that little church for quite a while. Did I mention the fact that the church was formerly built for The Church of Jesus Christ of Latter-day Saints? Its very cornerstone was etched with Mormon engravings for all to see. When I first discovered the church's history, I asked the young pastor if he had anointed the building and prayed over it. He smirked slightly and changed the subject. I took that as a no. Yet

another piece to the puzzle and another little squeeze
to the belly.

Worship services were very interesting at that little
church, to say the least. We were already somewhat con-
ditioned for these since we had survived the holy rolling
Baptist church shock show of 1993. We were growing in
our faith and open to whatever God was leading us to,
though not overly mature as far as Scripture knowledge
or the proper use thereof. I did, at the time, possess
more knowledge than I would have liked in the realm of
the supernatural due to my family's dysfunctional applications of it spanning decades and lifetimes. I was
also able to discern evil, familial spirits, and negative
spiritual influences from time to time and often in unexpected places.

My spidey senses tingling, I began to approach every Sunday service in hyper-alert mode. I wasn't exactly
watching the pastor through a critical lens back then,
though you could say I was in continual prayer and open
to receiving any type of sign God was willing to send
my way. I noticed an interesting consistency at every
single service. During prayer time, as with the previous church we had attended, people began to speak in
tongues. It wasn't "people"; it was one guy. Gerry. Gerry
spoke in tongues every single Sunday. Most often, it
was also Gerry who interpreted what the Lord was saying every single Sunday. Sometimes, a worship leader

would give an interpretation of Gerry's spiritual utterings, but it was often Gerry who did both. I also found it strange that to me, it sounded as if Gerry spoke the exact same syllables every single time the Holy Spirit overtook him with a message. I wholeheartedly believe in Holy Spirit-filled speaking in tongues as well as hearing and receiving its interpretation from the Lord. I've heard it throughout my life in various places from different reputable people, including my beautiful mother. When I had heard tongues spoken from others in the past, it never sounded the same and was never continually spoken and interpreted by the same person. Even though this weekly portrayal of the holiest members of the church flaunting their clearly spiritual superiority over the rest of us losers began to have some unwelcomed side-effects in my personal psyche, we continued to attend anyway.

The overall atmosphere of the church service had drastically shifted. It would be safe to say it felt as if the joy had totally left the building. I began to secretly dread attending each service but did so while channeling my inner early teenaged self's negative attitude about old fogeys and organized religion. I could honestly tell you that I sat in the pew, thinking about what I was going to make for Sunday dinner or where we could take the kids to eat after church. I doubt I heard a word the pastor said at that point in time and cringed every time Gerry began chanting in his boisterously loud and deep voice, professing God's timely message for the church.

On one particular Sunday, we arrived to discover that we were to have an elderly guest speaker and his wife in the place of our regular pastor, who had gone on vacation. The music was also different that day, as the regular worship leaders must have been out as well. The older pastor brought his guitar to the pulpit and sat on a stool as his sweet little wife stood beside him, hands folded in front of her with a beautiful smile on her face. They began to sing some older Christian country songs, and the strangest thing happened. I was watching the couple perform when I began to see two golden glowing figures standing behind them. The figures seem to be swaying side to side while clapping their hands. I blinked several times, looked around the room, then looked back up at the couple who were still singing. The angels were still there. I thought about telling my husband what I was seeing but figured he wouldn't believe me, so I remained quiet. I felt a prompting to mention it anyway, so I finally leaned over and quietly asked, "Do you see anything strange at the front of the room?" "No," he replied. "What do you see?" I proceeded to tell him and made it clear I didn't see faces, etcetera, only the golden glow of beings happily swaying in time to the music while clapping their hands. I was still not totally convinced in what I thought I had been seeing.

The song ended, and the pastor began to speak. The topic of discussion that Sunday, backed by scripture after scripture? Angels and ministering spirits. Seriously! The pastor went on to say that God's angels were present and with us in the room that very day, as my husband slowly turned his head in my direction with widened eyes and a grin forming on his face. You see, I had to tell him what I had witnessed at the very moment it was happening; otherwise, it would have been harder for him to believe me. God prompted me to speak, and though reluctant, I did as He wanted. That was part of His plan. He wanted us to see and feel the difference between a place filled with the Holy Spirit and a place completely lacking in His presence.

That was the very last time I ever saw or felt the spirit of the Lord in that small Virginian church. Consequently, we left it a short time after.

We learned many lessons from them, however. A major one being that just because someone sounds as if they are hearing from heaven and speaking in tongues doesn't necessarily mean that they are filled with the Holy Spirit or that God's spirit Himself is behind such utterings. As mentioned before, things are not always as they seem. We need to discern between what is and is not from the Lord.

Up until that time, while we were attending church, I remember sitting in the congregation wondering what was wrong with me? Those who were weekly speaking in tongues loudly in church and were interpreting their own utterings must truly have a closer relationship to the Lord. He seemed to be favoring them with majorly supernatural heavenly insight and blessings in abundance. Why wasn't I hearing from Him or growing closer to Him? What was wrong with me, and would God ever be able to use me? I felt defeated and confused. That should have been my second clue that all may not have been right with the church we had so loved in the beginning. We know that God is not the author of confusion; the devil is. First Corinthians 14:33 (AMP) states, "[f]or God [who is the source of their prophesying] is not a God of confusion and disorder but of peace and order. As [is the practice] in all churches of the saints (God's people)." We are also assured that God shows no favoritism as is so simply stated in Romans 2:11, "For God does not show favoritism." Clear, precise, and final. I was feeling condemnation for all the baggage and negative feelings that were building up while attending that church and was second-guessing myself and my motives at every turn. Romans 8:1 tells us, "Therefore, there is no condemnation for those who are in Christ Jesus." I'm pretty sure I knew that even way back then, but was also receiving darts from the enemy left, right, and sideways and, for some reason, was allowing him to gain the upper hand.

I truly believe that things had to unfold the way they did so that the Lord could teach me some valuable lessons as I grew in my walk with Him. He never left me and, in fact, began to work on my heart, opening my eyes as to the things that were not right in my own life and that seemed to be slightly off in that specific Pentecostal church. Quite honestly, we were both operating outside of God's will at that moment in time. I was developing a hyper-critical spirit towards the church and its tongue-toting parishioner, and the spirit leading the church in worship and interpretations did not seem to be from the Holy Spirit at all. Looking back, I can see the spirits of confusion and pride that seemed to dominate the church to be, in fact, numbers one and two on the devil's greatest hits parade.

Speaking in tongues is a special gift from the Holy Spirit and I, for one, am not against this amazing gift in any way. I know of many wonderful people who speak it fluently, regularly, and are filled with God's love and sweet spirit. Speaking in another tongue is a way for us to worship the Lord or pray when we give ourselves over to the Holy Spirit and His promptings. It edifies us supernaturally and takes over our prayer life, especially when we don't know what to pray or who to pray for. His spirit gives us a direct line to our heavenly Father. How awesome is that! "For anyone who speaks in a tongue does not speak to men but to God. Indeed, no one understands him; he utters mysteries with his spirit" (1 Corinthians 14:2).

I love how Paul writes in 1 Corinthians 14:19, "But in the church I would rather speak five intelligent words to instruct others than ten thousand words in a tongue." Of course, I am drawn to Paul's words due in part to the cymbal clanging, possibly un-spiritual, utterances I was hearing regularly from the aforementioned church services. There is a distinct difference in the sound of one speaking in tongues in complete surrender to the Lord for His glory, as opposed to one who is loudly parading a supposed gift for self-gratification, personal gain, or for spiritual importance within the church. In a place where such utterings show your high level of spiritual maturity above all others, that little church ate it up while allowing the speaker an elevated platform on all religious matters. After all, he was continually hearing from the Lord, wasn't he?

I am reminded of a quote a well-known Bible teacher has stated many times in her services. She mentions that "just because you go to church doesn't mean you're a Christian. I can go sit in my garage all day, and it doesn't make me a car." She's absolutely right on that one. This statement also unveiled another simple truth to me while attending that church. Just because someone may utter seemingly spiritual syllables loudly doesn't mean they are speaking in tongues as given by the Holy Spirit. Speaking in tongues may or not be utterances by our beloved Holy Spirit. They can, in fact, be from another supernatural spiritual influence altogether. Up until that point, I had no idea that people could speak in tongues with interpretation while operating in divination, witchcraft, or hearing from familial spirits instead of from the Lord. That could be why tongues sounded the same every single time they were spoken or why the same person, the speaker himself, was the only one interpreting.

Paul also discusses speaking in tongues in the love chapter of the Bible, 1 Corinthians 13:1, "If I speak in the tongues of men and of angels, but have not love, I am only a resounding gong or a clanging cymbal." There were numerous times in that small church when the spiritual tongues spoken at almost deafening decibels sounded as Paul had stated in that very scripture. As time went on, it was evident to me that the pastor, himself, did not appear to have been walking in genuine love for his sheep or the congregation that he was in charge of leading. If one decides to be a pastor, it is imperative that he or she has the heart and love of their heavenly Father, especially for their own flock.

Though I cannot pretend to know the genuine heart of the person who spoke in tongues on a continual basis at that little southern church, I can only recount the quickening I felt in my own spirit every time he spoke, and the gentle nudge assuring me that something was not right. I felt the Lord might have been showing me that he was no longer abiding in that place, and it was time for my family to move on.

So, what about the gift of speaking in tongues? Does everyone who accepts Jesus as their Lord and Savior and who has been filled with His Holy Spirit automatically speak in tongues? If one believes to have been filled with the Holy Spirit and does not receive the gift of speaking in tongues, does that mean he or she was not really filled with the Holy Spirit after all? Or maybe his or her faith was not large enough to receive the gift? Let's dissect this phenomenon via scripture and a specific case study, shall we?

First, we know that there are many different gifts of the Holy Spirit including, but not limited to the gift of speaking in tongues.

> To one there is given through the Spirit the message of wisdom, to another the message of knowledge by means of the same Spirit, to another faith by the same Spirit, to another gifts of healing by that one Spirit, to another miraculous powers, to another prophecy, to another distinguishing between spirits, to another speaking in different kinds of tongues, and to still another the interpreta-

tion of tongues. All these are the work of one and the same Spirit, and he gives them to each one, just as he determines.

1 Corinthians 12:8-11

These scriptures explain that there are many different gifts administered from the Holy Spirit Himself to each one of us as He wishes. He alone decides which of His gifts would work out best for each individual life and then graciously envelops us with them when He believes that we are mature enough to receive and utilize them properly.

I completely acknowledge that all gifts from the Holy Spirit are true, just, and available to any child of God who diligently seeks Him and accepts His Son, Jesus, as Savior and Lord. God made it clear that He does not show favoritism and that what He does for one, He will do for another.

In 1 Corinthians 14:5, Paul mentions, "I would like every one of you to speak in tongues, but I would rather have you prophesy. He who prophesies is greater than the one who speaks in tongues unless he interprets, so that the church may be edified."

I find it particularly interesting in the above scripture that Paul wishes all of us to be filled with the Holy Spirit and to speak in tongues. He also stated that the ability to translate or explain the message spoken in tongues to be especially important, which checks off both boxes for the tongue-speakers in the previously mentioned church. I absolutely loved the Amplified Bible's interpretation of the ending of that scripture in 1 Corinthians 14, "[s]o that the church may be edified [instructed, improved, strengthened]." This translation emphasized that the message from such an utterance must edify, improve, and strengthen the church. The act of speaking in and interpreting tongues should encourage and build up the church instead of disrupting true worship while instilling chaos and confusion in its wake.

It is my opinion that the small Virginian church we attended, though thankful for my husband's salvation and all the lessons learned from it, was slightly tipped to the supernaturally dysfunctional side of the scale. In this case, the dysfunctionality was not necessarily a good thing as it turned many away from its doors and may have caused several to become estranged from the church or their faith altogether. Not all Assemblies of God or Pentecostal churches are the same, as we've attended several throughout the years that were entirely spirit-filled and led as well. I sincerely and wholeheartedly support any denomination that is Bible-based, with Jesus as the head of the church.

We need to remember, as Paul notated, "[f]or God [who is the source of their prophesying] is not a God of

SUPERNATURALLY DYSFUNCTIONAL

confusion and disorder but of peace and order" (1 Corinthians 14:33, AMP). We always need to test and discern the spirits in order to avoid deception, which is not
always obviously or easily done.

When the day of Pentecost came in the Bible, according to Luke in Acts 2:3-4, "They saw what seemed to be
tongues of fire that separated and came to rest on each
of them. All of them were filled with the Holy Spirit and
began to speak in other tongues as the Spirit enabled
them." The scripture went on to say that a crowd began
to form, containing people from various lands who were
surprised that these Galileans were all speaking in their
own native languages. The Holy Spirit was ministering
to the people surrounding those who were speaking in
tongues in order that the unbelievers in the gathering
could be encouraged and hopefully ultimately receive
salvation. Speaking in tongues at this time in the Bible
had a purpose, which was to minister to those in need
as well as to worship and praise the Lord. The tongues
spoken and given by the Holy Spirit were not lifeless re-
petitive syllables but were actual words that edified and
changed lives. Nothing is ever wasted with God. His
words are true, life-affirming, life-giving, and always
have a purpose.

To make my final point and end an already lengthy
chapter, I need to transport you back in time to the late
1970s to the early 1980s and tell you about an elderly

retired Methodist minister by the name of Reverend Koehbler. The reverend resembled a cross between a Keebler elf character and Mr. Magoo. That may give you some insight as to how old I was at the time of these memories. He was my favorite minister. I loved it when he was the guest speaker at our church on Sundays. He had the most gentle and sweetest voice I had ever heard. The man oozed Jesus, as he would tell a story and then say, "Oh beloved," to get his point across. I always sat glued to the edge of my seat, hanging on to every single word. When you were around him, you just smiled and truly felt God's anointing presence surrounding him. His wife was just as sweet, very tiny, and always had a smile on her face. I remember visiting their home with my parents one sunny afternoon, sitting in their parlor, eating cookies, and chatting happily. Their room was baby blue in color, and adorning almost every wall and space, were the many faces of Jesus. They had more varied pictures of Jesus than I could even begin to count as a child. He collected them and must have received many as gifts. How could Reverend Koehbler and his adorable bride not ooze Jesus since Jesus was, in fact, seen on almost every wall of their home? There's a lesson in that scene alone, having the anointing of Jesus covering every single wall of our own homes may help to ensure peace, unspeakable joy, and divine protection.

Let the record show that our sweet Reverend Koehbler never spoke in tongues. Gasp! Does that mean that he wasn't truly filled with the Holy Spirit? How could he be if he never spoke in tongues? Many by today's holy-rolling standards would say you need to be baptized in the Holy Spirit, which I would agree with. But they also add, right along with being filled with the Holy Spirit, that all need to acquire the evidence of speaking in tongues to truly be an effective minister or preacher and to be most powerfully used by God. I beg to disagree on the speaking in tongues part. You catch more flies with honey, and my favorite minister was dripping with the sweetness of the Holy Spirit. He encouraged and affected all of us, whoever had the privilege of hearing him speak or of having known him. He left this world with a lasting legacy of love. If you met him once, I'm convinced, you saw the face of Jesus on this earth and felt his unconditional love. In the well-known actual "Love Chapter" of the Bible, 1 Corinthians 13, Paul explains to us that the greatest thing we can do is to love. The reverend and Mrs. Koehbler exemplified the picture Paul painted for us and finished their race and purpose on this earth with great grace, filled to overflowing with God's Holy Spirit. You will never convince me otherwise. He was filled with the Holy Spirit and functioned incredibly well on this earth with God's supernatural approval and guidance.

10

Paranormal Perplexities

A book on supernatural happenings, dysfunctional or otherwise, cannot be written, in my opinion, without including the ghost hunting phenomena that has swept the world for decades. In fact, ghost stories have spanned the globe for hundreds and even thousands of years in every culture. The Bible itself tells of a ghostly appearance witnessed by Saul in the Old Testament, as well as Jesus mistakenly being identified as a ghost by His very own disciples on a later occasion in the New Testament. This would lead me to believe that even during biblical times, there were ghostly discussions happening, at least to some degree.

I find it fascinating to note that many of us will pay good money to be scared either at the movies, in a haunted house or escape room, on a haunted hayride, or on a ghost tour. The spookier, the better. And when the Halloween season arrives, all bets are off on the scare-your-pants-off meter. Brothers, sisters, cousins, and friends have been trying to find new ways of scaring each other quite possibly for as long as they've known each other. I am no exception.

You already know a little about my history and that I could already have been predisposed to a fascination with the supernatural, most likely due to my bloodline. I'm not going to lie. I loved a good ghost story as a kid. Since I believed to have seen a few specters in my formative years, I wanted to test the waters whenever I got the chance to find out if I could see even more.

I grew up in a small town and rode my bicycle everywhere I went. Do you remember back when it was safe for children to ride their bikes without adult supervision, unlike today? On one happy summer day, I took a ride downtown to hang out with a young friend, who just happened to live close to an abandoned hospital building. We proceeded to do what any un-supervised ten-year-old would do. We found a way in. No specter chased us or tried to invade our personal space at any time during our quest through the forbidden zone, though I can tell you that we walked through several extremely cold spots along the way. This seemed slightly strange to us since it was, at that specific time, the middle of summer and extremely hot and humid. According to most ghost hunting or paranormal investigators, cold spots are believed to be indicative of supernaturally ghostly manifestations in that specific area. Thank goodness we were not privy to that information during our little expedition through the abandoned hospital and happily wandered on. I remember it seeming especially chilly in the nursery, where I personally had spent the beginning of my journey on the planet, as did most who lived in my tiny town. We didn't stay in the old hospital for very long and exited without incident. To this day, I still can't believe I made that excursion at such a young age without an injury or jail time of any kind. My guardian angel was most definitely on overtime throughout my entire childhood.

As a teenager, my friends and I frequented cemeteries, abandoned and condemned rural farmhouses, and creepy woods or roads where the popular ghostly lights or even the urban legend of Sister Sarah dressed in white were known to appear. Being the noisy, irreverent, and obnoxious teenagers that we were, we never uncovered anything supernatural but did manage to try to tip a cow or two along the way. It is amazing that I survived my teenage years at all. I'm convinced that many teenagers are slightly lacking in the common-sense arena, perhaps due to their hormonal overload. I know I was one suffering the same affliction. I remain extremely thankful for a praying mother and the protective angels she sent my way.

Imagine my surprise, many years later, when my own teenagers asked to go on ghost tours and haunts while on various vacations. My kids loved a good scare, so we obliged them on occasion. They did experience a little ghostly activity here and there, at least enough to hold their interest, while I appreciated the types of tours that were more historically based. If any paranormal activity appeared to be present during these excursions, it was most likely due to familiar spirits or demonic entities, which, in my opinion, belong to the extremely dysfunctional end of the supernatural pendulum.

Still, for some strange reason, on these ghost hunts, I was often the one who received the supernatural attention. Perhaps the familiar spirits loved a challenge or wished to change my point of view on the matter of their existence. The electromagnetic field detector (EMF) could be quiet for several others who were hunting in the same room, while mine would be the only one that went off when it was asked a question. On another occasion, I felt a tap on the top of my head as the tour guide smiled and told me that was a common occurrence. As the same haunted tour progressed, and while snapping lots of pictures in succession rapidly, we saw a person right in front of me with her brown hair flowing in the wind in one shot for a split second in a frame. The very next shot taken immediately following in the exact same spot showed that nothing was there. There was no wind in the attic, and no one else was in that exact area of the room. In my opinion, it would seem that when someone is open to see or experience so-called ghost encounters, the supernatural may then oblige and manifest itself.

The previous examples of a few ghost experiences occurred most likely because all willing participants involved were actively seeking out a supernatural experience. I'm relatively sure that we all already have demonic entities specifically assigned to each one of us, instructed to do whatever they can to find a portal into our homes and lives on any given day. These ghosts in the machine may find a foothold or entry point into our homes due in part to some of the programs we watch on the internet or television as well as through songs designed for demonic attachment. Though it may seem hard to believe in the natural, I can assure you of its validity. For example, soft pornography, prevalent in most programming nowadays, when willingly viewed in the home or at the movies, can trigger a possible addiction to pornography in the future. The Christian church is not immune to such addiction issues, and many of its leaders have fallen out of favor due to its devastating grip. How do you think it all began? This obviously doesn't happen to every single person who watches shows or movies that are for mature audiences only, but you had better believe that seeds are being planted and when roots develop, evil results may be imminent. Unwanted doors can and most likely will then be opened to the supernatural. The enemy hates your family. Mature-themed programming can be a sneaky way for him to gain a stronghold into your life and wreak havoc on otherwise healthy relationships.

Similarly, when horror movies or movies riddled with satanic symbols, incantations, or supernaturally evil rituals are viewed once or on a regular basis, enormous unwanted doors will be opened. Satan is a deceiver and often disguises himself as a harmless being of light. One of his greatest deceptions is to convince many that he does not even exist or that watching such things will not affect the viewer in any unhealthy way. When viewings of all-out evil are consumed, however, by the eyes and taken in by the ears, it may become open season on the wicked consequences of our choices to let them in by our viewership. Whether you believe it or not, the devil has that right, regardless of your opinions on his existence. You have given it to him by watching such programs or by buying and listening to demonic-filled music regularly. Then the real battle begins. You need to understand that the battle is for your soul, and he is deceptively convincing. He has studied you since the day you were born and knows your weaknesses. You play right into his hands when being a willing participant in the unhealthy choices you make.

Funnily enough, computer programmers have been known to use the phrase "ghost in the machine" to describe when a program runs the opposite of their expectations. They're not wrong as far as the demonic presence of ghosts that may already be in our personal home machines. We could use the very same terminology to describe what often comes out of our computer, television, or phone screen regularly. When we neglect to pay attention to the actual content of what we watch or listen to and even have it playing just for sound in a room, we may be inviting the ghost in the machine to drop in and make itself at home. In this case, however, it's not Casper, the friendly ghost, making his daily rounds, spreading sunshine and cheer. It is most likely a demonic entity, instead, trying to gain an entry into your life.

At this point in my writing, I feel prompted to express a little disclaimer regarding all you have read so far. It is not my intention to persuade the reader to conform to my specific beliefs or to deflate any personal balloons of those who regularly engage in ghostly hunts or haunts. I can only write about personal encounters and what I've found to be true in the case of my family, as well as the fires we've all walked through. Though these seemingly harmless programs, tours, movies, or songs may appear relatively risk-free, it has been my experience that they are, in reality, anything but harmless in nature. The open doorways we create for ourselves can easily cause evil attachments that will eventually show their true colors. If you don't know the signs and don't have the faith or tools for protection, you may be prone to some miserable repercussions. My goal is to arm you, as best as I can, so that you don't have to live in torment and will be able to protect yourself and your loved ones.

Do you remember the story of my demon-possessed cousin? The demons screamed that they gained a stronghold over her from the television programs of the day. One demon even mentioned the title of a well-known cartoon that kept her child-minded and unable to learn, as well as "those filthy, lusty soap operas." It verbally and loudly quoted those things, using many intelligent words that were not even in my cousin's limited vocabulary. Stuff just got real.

I find it extremely interesting that we have seen a continual and alarming climb in the number of paranormal reality shows on the internet and television over the past several years. Though most of these programs are scripted and rigged for suspense as well as shock value, many are faked and staged to fuel our curiosity and keep us coming back for more. It was also evident, in several programs, that the well-meaning paranormal investigators would end the show by empathizing with the family or people being tormented, affirming that they did indeed have some type of ghostly or paranormal problem, and would proceed to just leave them without eliminating their supernatural tormentor. I found it strange that these people were advised to make peace with their haunting, as their particular ghost was not harmful or mean-spirited in any way. Some found comfort in just knowing that they had a spirit in the house that wasn't evil and that all would be well with it hanging around. After all, the reality television paranormal investigators were unlike the classic original *Ghostbusters* and most likely did not have their own ghost-containment system. On a couple of varied shows, however, the ghost hunters would offer a priest for an exorcism or cleansing ritual, or perhaps a medium armed with sage and sheer willpower to rid the affected area or family of their paranormal problem. People seem to be eating this stuff up. They must be because there appears to be a growing number of these paranormal shows appearing almost daily. Add to that the constant ghostly activity that everyday people, armed with unedited iPhones and home security cameras, are catching and loading onto social media platforms continually. Some of these credible sources lead me to believe that the supernatural has been manifesting more often, as of late, and evil appears to be getting bolder. Dissecting this growing phenomenon is not as complicated as it may sometimes seem, and the simplest answer is often the most accurate.

The dictionary, according to Merriam-Webster[4], defines the word "ghost" as "a disembodied soul, a spirit, or a demon." The basic definition, according to many paranormal investigators, would lead us to believe that ghosts are, in fact, a person's spirit that continues to exist in some form after the physical body has died. They also believe that these so-called ghosts attain the ability to appear to unsuspecting humans by receiving energy from electromagnetic fields caused by machines and electricity prevalent in our homes and buildings.

Some scientists have indicated that it would be next to impossible to prove that something, whether paranormal or ghost-like in nature, does not actually exist. Some were also known to suppose that the mere belief in the supernatural or paranormal to be a dangerous one. Several scientists even seem to be of the opinion that individuals who believe in ghosts or supernatural activity may suffer a reduction in the ability to make rational day-to-day decisions. It was suggested that those of us who have had personal otherworldly encounters might be prone to lose touch with reality or be unable to discern it from fantasy. To quote my favorite Vulcan Chief Science Officer, "Fascinating."

---

4 www.merriam-webster.com

Nevertheless, you can google all kinds of information about ghost sightings, stories, or paranormal activity and come up with endless possibilities of how to conjure up your own personal supernatural experience. Ghosts even seem to have their own classifications. For example, a poltergeist, which in German means a "knocking spirit," is supposedly a phenomenon that occurs when telekinetic energy from an angry or frustrated person/teenager is released, usually while they are fast asleep during their dream cycle, to wreak its havoc on the living. To visualize this, it may help to consider the obscurus character in an extremely popular wizarding movie series. I wonder how many poltergeists, by the above definition, I could have personally, unknowingly, and telekinetically set free while sleeping due to the frustrations of the day? By that very definition, there should be tons of poltergeists making messes all over the globe at this very moment, originating from angsty, sleeping teenagers. That alone could cause the end of the world as we know it if it were a true phenomenon.

Residual hauntings are supposedly the most common and are believed to replay the same scene over and over as a movie in a continual loop. An example could include an old museum where people see some type of apparition manifest at a certain time of the day or night in the same area as if the person who passed is still going through the normal actions of their previous life or

SUPERNATURALLY DYSFUNCTIONAL

perhaps reliving the way they died over and over, for all eternity.

An intelligent haunting, according to the ghost hunting experts, has more to do with the entity interacting with occupants or investigators when asked to prove their presence. Though to be fair, intelligent hauntings, or familiar spirits, at a person's home or place of business will act out at different times to scare or get someone's attention. Let the record show that if I were being haunted at any given time, I would probably not take the time to ask the spirit harassing me a question or ask them if they could make a noise for me. Though I must confess, while gathering information for this part of my story, I did download a couple of ghost-hunting phone applications to test the waters. One specific notable interest was the program that supposedly gathers words on your phone from a spirit in your home or area. Words did congregate on my screen, but only when in my garage. They were vague but virtually deceptive words that could mean whatever you imagined or gave meaning to. Upon re-entering my house and leaving the garage, the word that appeared was "fade," and I was a little amused. The words also appeared on my phone screen while in areas that had higher electromagnetic fields, which obviously affected the algorithm of the phone application. My house had already been blessed and anointed with oil everywhere except in the garage. I do not put much stock into phone applications, but you can see that the enemy can try to manipulate us in little ways meant to scare or intrigue us. As we give more life to the possibility of supernatural encounters or wish to find more words from the supernatural side of our reality by using a phone application, we could be at risk of opening another unwanted and wicked door. It can be tempting, though, especially in the name of research. This would most definitely be the epitome of an intelligent haunting by professional standards, as the reality shows convey.

These shows also explain the existence of harmful ghost categories known as evil entities, which they claim may admittedly be demonic in nature and can sometimes lead to a possession. So, according to the professionals, only this specific classification could be demonic in nature. Really? Let's dig a little deeper to find the true origin of all paranormal or ghostly activity.

With the growing escalation of paranormal reality television shows of all kinds, along with inherently evil series and movies that unashamedly applaud the supernatural, evil appears to be getting bolder, flaunting its presence at every turn. The devil is unquestionably sneaky, cunning, and deceptive but doesn't even have to hide himself, as humans everywhere seem to celebrate and usher in evil themselves. We are making his job even easier by our personal life choices.

We know well that many religions describe an afterlife where spirits are sent to be rewarded or punished according to their deeds while alive on the earth. Some go so far as to believe, including most paranormal investigators, that spirits who fail to cross over into the afterlife remain on earth in ghostly form due to their own personal unfinished business. This would contradict what we are told in 2 Corinthians 5:8, "We are confident, I say, and would prefer to be away from the body and at home with the Lord." Paul makes it clear that when we die, and our spirit is then separated from the body, we will immediately be with the Lord in heaven if we believe in Jesus and live our lives accordingly. It is also believed that eternity will be spent in either heaven or hell, no lingering around on the earth until your unfinished business is resolved.

Though the word "ghost" does appear in the King James Version of the Bible 108 times, it is never used to describe the disembodied spirit of a deceased person. One of the first times it appeared in the Bible was in Genesis 25:8 in the King James Version and was quoted as stating, "Abraham gave up the ghost, and died in a good old age, an old man, and full of years; and was gathered to his people." In this scripture, giving up the ghost referred to the moment that the spirit left the body upon death and then traveled on to heaven or hell.

In Luke 16:22-23, Jesus said, "The time came when the beggar died and the angels carried him to Abraham's side. The rich man also died and was buried. In hell, where he was in torment, he looked up and saw Abraham far away, with Lazarus by his side." Jesus, the Lord Himself, said that when the beggar died, he immediately went to heaven. He did not pass go or collect two hundred dollars. Purgatory was not even mentioned. There was no visibly present barrier of any kind between heaven and hell in this scripture that blocked the rich man's view. As Lazarus was in heaven, chatting with Abraham, the rich man could see him from his tormented position in hell.

When one of the thieves on the cross next to Jesus asked the Lord to remember him when he went into His kingdom, Jesus answered him in Luke 23:43, "I tell you the truth, today you will be with me in paradise." There is no doubt that, according to Jesus, the thief on the cross beside Him was forgiven and went on to be with Him in heaven upon his death. He didn't linger on the earth with unresolved business to finish or wrongs to be made right in a ghostly body. He was simply in heaven.

Further proof that ghosts are not from deceased human beings can be found in Psalm 146:4. In this scripture, we are told, "When their spirit departs, they return to the ground; on that very day their plans come to nothing." Game over, man. There is no unfinished business to trap their souls in ghostly form on the earth until they rectify their wrongdoings.

In 1 Samuel 28:7-2, King Saul went out, in disguise, to find a medium known as "the Witch of Endor." He wanted to summon Samuel, a deceased and well thought of prophet. A ghost-like figure, who looked like Samuel, rose from the ground and scared the witch, who then fell at its feet. The Bible mentioned that Samuel, the spirit or ghost, answered the king. Many believe a familiar spirit, which is simply a specifically assigned demon or doppelganger, was impersonating Samuel. This may have been because the ghostly figure told King Saul that all his sons would die the very next day, though some actually survived. The ghostly prophet, known for his accuracy while alive, had been wrong on this specific prediction or prophecy. Saul sought out the occult, which was clearly condemned by God, who had warned us all about such things in His Word. Consequently, King Saul also died the day after conjuring up the dead prophet, along with many of his sons.

Leviticus 19:31 clearly states, "Do not turn to mediums or seek out spiritists, for you will be defiled by them. I am the Lord your God." God warns us that when we are open to hearing what mediums or spiritists tell us through the channeling of the demonic, we will then be defiled or ruined by them. This could lead to an eternity of separation from a loving God who wishes that none of us should perish. That is a gamble, in all honesty, that I am not willing to take.

King Saul seemed to have lost all reason or sanity in his quest to have Samuel summoned from the dead, as shown in the book of Samuel. He was obviously deceived and paid the ultimate price with his soul. In Deuteronomy, beginning in the ninth verse of chapter 18, we learn of practices that are detestable to the Lord. Saul actively pursued the occult, obviously rebelling against God. As a reminder notated in a previous chapter, Deuteronomy 18:10-12 clearly stated:

> Let no one be found among you who sacrifices his son or daughter in the fire, who practices divination or sorcery, interprets omens, engages in witchcraft, or casts spells, or who is a medium or spiritist or who consults the dead. Anyone who does these things is detestable to the Lord, and because of these detestable practices the Lord will drive out those nations before you.
>
> Deuteronomy 18:10-12

Saul willingly engaged in what was detestable in God's sight and ended up committing suicide after his loss to the Philistines.

Manasseh, the king of Judah, was most definitely evil in the sight of the Lord as well. We discover in 2 Kings 21:6, "He sacrificed his own son in the fire, practiced sorcery and divination, and consulted mediums and spiritists." He, too, provoked God to anger. I would personally rather stay in God's good graces instead of making Him angry on purpose, but that's just me.

Yes, it is possible that people may encounter a spirit or paranormal entity today, especially as the enemy has upped his game and is scrambling to entrap as many as he can before his ultimately lengthy stint in the fiery pit made especially for him. These chance meetings are most likely to be demonic in nature rather than ghostly. We know that demons are fallen angels that are governed by the devil, acting as familiar spirits who mimic the dead to deceive the living. That is why we are told in 1 John 4:1, "Dear friends, do not believe every spirit, but test the spirits to see whether they are from God, because many false prophets have gone out into the world."

At this point, you may be asking yourself how exactly can I test a spirit to discern if it is from God or the devil? I like the Amplified Bible's version of John's explanation to that very question. He writes:

By this you know and recognize the Spirit of God: every spirit that acknowledges and confesses [the fact] that Jesus Christ has [actually] come in the flesh [as a man] is from God [God is its source]; and every spirit that does not confess Jesus [acknowledging that He has come in the flesh, but would deny any of the Son's true nature] is not of God; this is the spirit of antichrist, which you have heard is coming, and is now already in the world.

John 4:2-3 (AMP)

Though the devil and his demons may disguise themselves as something heavenly, when asked if they love Jesus or believe He is Lord, Savior, and the true Son of God, they will deny Him, most likely in a profane manner.

For many of us, it is difficult to understand how intelligent people on the earth today could deny Jesus, speak and do evil while blaspheming His name, denounce Him as Savior, and willingly decide to follow the devil and occult or New Age practices. People still do so proudly. Evidence of this type of fascination continues to grow at an alarmingly increased rate more and more every day. First Timothy 4:1 tells us, "The Spirit clearly says that in later times some will abandon the faith and follow deceiving spirits and things taught by demons." These deceiving and familiar spirits have one agenda, to get God's people distracted from the truth of His

Word so that we will fall away from God and His salvation. You could think of Satan's plan for our destruction as going along with that old saying, "Misery loves company." You had better believe that he is miserable and defeated, as he already knows the end of his story. That still will not keep him from using every trick in his arsenal to take as many of us with him as he can.

In Isaiah 8:19, it is written, "When men tell you to consult mediums and spiritists, who whisper and mutter, should not a people inquire of their God? Why consult the dead on behalf of the living?" That's a truly valid question, yet some people do the very thing that we are warned against.

The dead know nothing, which we find in Ecclesiastes 9:5-6, "For the living know that they will die, but the dead know nothing; they have no further reward, and even the memory of them is forgotten. Their love, their hate, and their jealousy have long since vanished; never again will they have a part in anything that happens under the sun." It is evident, according to these verses, that when we pass away, we are gone from this earth and have no further knowledge or dealings with anything on it. Likewise, there are no spirits lingering as shadows or ghosts of loved ones who had once lived on the earth and have since passed away. Our spirit departs the earth as our earthly bodies remain as shells in the grave. The dead know nothing.

So, if that is true, how do we explain what goes on in supposed haunted houses? Can a home really be haunted? Well, according to Job in chapter 7, there can be no such thing as a haunted house or at least one inhabited by an actual ghost. We discover in Job 7:9-10, "As a cloud vanishes and is gone, so he who goes down to the grave does not return. He will never come to his house again; his place will know him no more." Therefore, ghosts cannot haunt any home or building. When we are dead, our spirit cannot return to our home, place of employment, favorite vacation spot, origin of death, or to harass loved ones and enemies. The Bible has made it clear that we will cease to exist on the earth, period.

For the sake of argument, let's refer to ghosts as familiar spirits and remind ourselves once again that Isaiah 8:19 asks, "Why consult the dead on behalf of the living?" Moving on to verse 20, we are told, "To the law and to the testimony! If they do not speak according to this word, they have no light of dawn." Isaiah goes on to say that those who decide to consult mediums, spiritists, witches, etcetera, will "see only distress and darkness, the gloom of anguish; and they will be driven away into darkness and overwhelming night," verse 22 (AMP). Notice it states that it is those who consult with, not just those who engage in occult practices, to be the ones who end up in darkness or hell. So merely going to a fortune teller or medium for fun not only widely opens doors for the enemy and his paranormal parade of minions, but it will also inevitably lead to a one-way ticket to midnight, eternally.

God made it clear in Leviticus 19:31 (AMP), "Do not turn to mediums [who pretend to consult the dead] or to spiritists [who have spirits of divination]; do not seek them out and be defiled by them. I am the Lord your God." Those who communicate or seek out the above-mentioned, working closely with familiar spirits of the enemy, will not be happy with their ending result.

Though I am no scholarly theologian or religious fanatic, I can honestly and openly share what I've learned through the inherent Word of God and through personal experience. The supernatural realm is even more real than our perceived reality of the world around us. You may be fooling yourself if you don't believe that it always surrounds us, even though we can't usually glimpse its workings with our own eyes. After all, you are a spirit being yourself living in a human body. If you are, at this point, still a bit skeptical and one who lives out the credo seeing is believing, take heart. You may eventually get exactly what you wish for, a chance to glimpse the supernatural. It is my hope, however, that going forward, you will not allow yourself to be easily manipulated into believing, as the ongoing ghost culture enthusiasts do, with reckless abandon.

Often, a ghostly or supernatural visitation stems from a familiar spirit sent to manipulate us. There can always be exceptions to this belief, as God is God and can do whatever He wants and use whoever He wants to lead, help, or comfort us, especially in times of desperation or intense and endless grief. I personally know of a couple of people who believed they had visitations from their deceased children. One had been praying to the Lord that He let her know her child was safe and in His care. Several nights after her prayer, her daughter appeared to be in the room with her. She didn't speak but only smiled in a way that her mother instantly knew she was okay. She sensed in her spirit that her daughter was also letting her know she couldn't stay. She believed that God heard and answered the prayer of a grieving mother and, in turn, received great peace from the event. She shared her story with others, much later, in the hopes that it encouraged and edified their belief in an eternity with God and deceased loved ones. It is not my place to judge or call every visitation a ploy from the enemy used to manipulate us. In the case of my friend, this strengthened her faith in God when it would have been all too easy for her to blame Him for the loss of her child. Not only did it build her faith, but also went on to bless many others who heard of her experience. I am positive the devil wouldn't want such encouraging publicity for God on his watch had he been the designer of that particular visitation. As with everything, we always test the spirits. A familiar spirit has evil intent, though it can be deceptively encouraging and may manifest on more than one occasion. My friend knew that this was a one-and-done episode and felt that God had answered prayer beyond legalistic convention. Please note that her experience is the exception and not the rule, as familiar spirits are usually the culprits of supposed divine visitations, as biblical scripture explained. In this exception, however, God did it His way. To me, this epitomizes the example of how much He truly loves each and every one of us. To meet us exactly where we are and when we need Him the most.

Again, dear reader, it is not my job to judge any experience that you or anyone else has gone through. Since I am receiving these stories second-hand, meaning I was not there in person to witness them, I can only express what the women who lived through the events or visitations experienced. I would also like to emphasize that both are devout Christians who do not seek out New Age or occult practices in any way. They are pure in heart and love the Lord even though they don't understand why such losses occurred to them.

We now know familiar spirit entities to be fallen angels sent to deceive us and on a mission from the devil himself, often appearing as lovely and caring. Second Corinthians 11:14-15 makes this point clear as Paul explains, "And no wonder, for Satan himself masquerades as an angel of light. It is not surprising, then, if his servants masquerade as servants of righteousness. Their end will be what their actions deserve."

John recorded in Revelation 12:9 (AMP), "And the great dragon was thrown down, the age-old serpent who is called the devil and Satan, he who continually deceives and seduces the entire inhabited world; he was thrown down to the earth, and his angels were thrown down with him." Evil spirits on the earth today are fallen angels who followed Satan when thrown out of heaven due to his rebellion against God. According to John, the devil's goal or job is to continually seduce and deceive us all. He is relentless in his tactics and goal-oriented with tunnel vision in his desire to wipe us out. He has no heart, no love, and cannot be reasoned with as he is a supernatural being and inhuman in every way. All he knows is hate, and he will do all he can to turn as many of us away from the Lord before his reign on the earth is through. He passionately hates and despises all that God loves. That includes me, and that includes you. Does that mean we need to live in fear of the devil's continual attacks or supernaturally paranormal manifestations? Let's find out what Jesus says on the matter.

When His disciples returned to Jesus after going out and following His instructions to proclaim His Word, heal the people, and cast out demons, they excitedly reported that even the demons had to submit to them when using His holy name. Jesus replied to them in Luke 10:18-20, "I saw Satan fall like lightning from heaven. I have given you authority to trample on snakes and scorpions and to overcome all the power of the enemy; nothing will harm you. However, do not rejoice that the spirits submit to you, but rejoice that your names are written in heaven."

Jesus made it clear that He gave us the authority to overcome all the power of the enemy by using His name. The devil and his demons are already beaten under our feet and must always submit to us in the name of Jesus. Many are unaware of this amazing truth and live a defeated life, allowing the devil to have his way. We have good reason not to live afraid according to Romans 8:31, "What then shall we say in response to this? If God is for us, who can be against us?" God is for us, and we have overcome the enemy because of the authority His only begotten Son, Jesus, gave to each one of us. It's up to us to actively utilize the authority we've already been given.

Paul goes on to tell us in Romans 8:37, "No, in all these things we are more than conquerors through him who loved us." We can confidently overcome the enemy because we are more than conquerors due to the undeniable fact that Jesus loved us so much that He willingly went to the cross to give us that authority. Jesus reminded us, however, that we should not be happy about having dominion over evil but instead should be overflowing with joy because our names are written in heaven.

Paul ends this chapter beautifully as he explains in Romans 8:38-39, "For I am convinced that neither death nor life, neither angels nor demons, neither the present nor the future, nor any powers, neither height nor depth nor anything else in all creation, will be able to separate us from the love of God that is in Christ Jesus our Lord." I take great comfort in those scriptures, and I wish the same for you; how encouraging to know that absolutely nothing could ever separate us from God's love.

Knowing that you have complete power over a manifesting apparition or ramblings of all demonic activity that could dare to cross your path either now or in the future should hopefully bring you a sense of peace. Whether you feel Him or not, the Lord and His angels are always around you for divine protection against anything the enemy tries to throw at you. They are patiently waiting and longing to help you when you cry out to God for help. All you have to do is call on the name of Jesus: "For, 'Everyone who calls on the name of the Lord will be saved'" (Romans 10:13). Ask, believe, receive. It really is that simple.

11

Dream a Little Dream

Have you ever had a dream that, upon waking, you just couldn't seem to shake? Did its symbols continue to flood your mind as you began your morning routine, only to wonder its possible meaning? Do you ever think of such dreams as the aftermath of eating too much pizza or one glass of wine too many before bedtime? If you answered yes to any of the previous questions, you might take some solace in the fact that you are not alone. We all dream; there's no denying it. Some have the luxury of forgetting most of their dreams before waking in the morning. My husband comes to mind on that one, unlike myself. I dream constantly, though I sometimes only remember its fragments. Sometimes, it's the fragments that turn out to be the most significant or endearing.

If we sleep around eight hours or one-third of the day, we will ultimately spend close to a third of our lives asleep. So, by the time we reach the age of seventy-five, we will have spent twenty-five years or 9,125 days sleeping. According to the National Institute of Health[5], the average person dreams around four to six times a night and may even spend as much as two hours dreaming during that time. If we spend that many days asleep, multiplied by around two hours of nightly dreaming, that equals an incredible amount of our lifetime where dreaming takes center stage. Odds are also pretty good that we will remember at least a few of them.

A dream, according to Merriam Webster, is "a series of thoughts, images, or emotions occurring during sleep." Obviously, dreams are usually stories that don't always seem to make sense to us afterward. Whimsical or nonsensical themes may be exactly what makes them fun, interesting, and more of a challenge to try to figure out.

Some scientific researchers believe that our dreams act as the go-between for our memories and moods, helping to regulate them both. Many consider our dreams to be a type of overnight therapy. According to that line of thought, to be sleep deprived would mean we could be dream deprived as well. Going without restorative sleep is known to be detrimental to our health. Dream deprivation could also cause similar issues, as the subconscious mind has no way to express itself or

5 www.healthline.com

work out the stressful feelings that may be causing certain types of repression or emotional blockages during waking life. Dreams may range from normal and ordinary to exciting, adventurous, or even to the slightly bizarre.

The very first dreams ever actually recorded occurred in Mesopotamia over 5,000 years ago and were discovered by archaeologists on clay tablets. During ancient Roman and Greek times, dreams were believed to have derived directly as downloads from their deities or deceased people and were thought to predict the future. Some ancient cultures actively practiced dream incubation with the intention of cultivating prophetic types of dreams.

According to Sigmund Freud, our dreams simply reveal our hidden emotions and desires. Other theories believe dreams aid in problem-solving, the formation of memories, or that they occur due to random brain stimulation. In general, many people endorse the Freudian theory of dreams and their meaning.

Some people today do not believe that dreams have any kind of meaning at all, however, and that trying to decipher them would be a waste of valuable time. I don't particularly fall into the unbelief category, though I've had some doozies in the dream realm that shadow the sentiment. I do believe that our dream life can be a way for God to communicate with us, send us warnings, or give us an idea of the path we need to follow in our waking reality. In that regard, since we are, in fact, spiritual beings living in a physical body, dreams can be functionally helpful messages from our supernatural father in heaven. Likewise, dreams could be majorly supernaturally dysfunctional in nature when emanating from the devil and his cohorts, especially when we give our time and attention to them.

When Joel 2:28 talks about the day of the Lord, he tells us, "And afterward, I will pour out my Spirit on all people. Your sons and daughters will prophesy, your old men will dream dreams, your young men will see visions." Luke repeated Joel's scripture in Acts 2:17, "In the last days, God says, I will pour out my Spirit on all people. Your sons and daughters will prophesy, your young men will see visions, your old men will dream dreams." In case you haven't been keeping up with the 2020-21 COVID-19 current events, we are presently in Joel's "day of the Lord," which correlates with Luke's "in the last days" quote. Many Christians would agree that we are in the days leading up to the second coming of the Lord on the earth. Though, to be fair, Christians have believed us to be in the last days since Jesus went to the cross and was resurrected. Dreams and prophecies currently bombard us at every turn on emails, social media, television, and in our churches. In fact, as I am finishing up this chapter, I have discovered an endless number of people all over the world who insist that they are having rapture or end of the world dreams and that Jesus has told them personally, He is coming back soon. All you have to do is go to YouTube and search "rapture dreams" to find countless videos of ordinary people relaying their urgent messages on the subject.

First of all, we know that God's timing is not our own timing. He has been telling His people to be ready for the return of His Son since the resurrection. He has also made it clear to us that no one knows the exact day or time of His return, not even the Son Himself. We are told in Matthew 24:36, "But about that day or hour no one knows, not even the angels in heaven, nor the Son, but only the Father."

One particularly distressed dreamer noted that in her dream, Jesus told her to warn the people on earth, "My father will be sending Me down at any moment now, because He is very angry with all that is happening on the earth, how people are behaving, and won't allow it to go on for much longer. They must be ready for My return." Well, I can't begin to know or judge the accuracy of such dreams without my own personal; let's just wait and see attitude. I'm sure, upon her waking, the dream would have caused a sense of urgency and panic in the heart of the dreamer. In fact, all that she felt and shared could very well be what the Lord is trying to warn us about, as it most definitely would make sense with all the ugliness of life on the planet at this very moment in history. One thing is apparent, this young lady wholeheartedly believes all of it and is bravely sharing it via video to as many as will watch and listen.

We believe that God is perfectly able to download dreams into our subconscious while we sleep if He desires to. He can also give us a vision, allowing us to look into another realm while awake, just as previously mentioned scriptures would imply. We've established the probability that all people dream, regardless of their ability to fully recall it once awake. Do all dreams originate from God, wanting to send important messages or warnings down to earth, or can some be used for evil intentions? Allow me to answer with a definite yes, on both counts. Our dreams could be supernaturally functional when they allow us a glimpse into a type of message or warning from the Lord. On the flip side, they can be supernaturally dysfunctional when originating from the evil side of the spectrum in order to confuse, manipulate, or even weaken your faith walk.

If you dare to humor me for a few more moments of your time, I'd like to share a couple of my own dreams as an example of how God could be working in our lives. Within a handful of exceptions, my dreams may consist of crazy places I've never been with people I've never met or just plain strange scenarios in general. Usually, in waking from such dreams, a few key things or items will stand out to me and linger for a time. Here is an excerpt from one dream in particular:

I Dream in French

Last night I had a dream that I was meant to share. While sitting at the piano with my daughter, I heard a voice say, *"Suis Moi, Terres."* After hearing it, I repeated it twice, and guess since I had no idea of its meaning, I woke up. It was around 3 a.m.-ish. To the best of my ability, I typed into my phone what I had heard, thinking I'd look it up in the morning. Please know, I do not speak or understand French; I haven't watched any French movies with subtitles and have never heard these words until my dream.

Upon researching these words, I discovered that *suis moi* meant "follow me" and that *terres* meant "land." When I looked up the word *terres*, pictures of lands and of the world popped up.

Every so often, God winks, and many times, I'm sad to say I've missed it.

He also has an awesome sense of humor, knowing how much I enjoy the challenge of trying to decode some of my wacky dreams. I did promise that I would share whatever He put on my heart in the hopes that He could use even me.

So today, I'm sharing what I dreamt and pray that it blesses you. It's a pretty simple message.

He wants us (the world) to follow Him and to seek His face in the middle of all of that is happening around us today.

Second Chronicles 7:14 tells us, "Then if my people who are called by my name will humble themselves and pray and seek my face and turn from their wicked ways, I will hear from heaven and will forgive their sin and will heal their land."

We, as humans, make it complicated. It's not. Pray, follow, believe. He's winking. He'll never leave you. He loves you.

When I got up the next morning, I wrote and publicly posted the dream on social media, which I don't often do. I usually keep dreams somewhat private and share them only if I feel led to do so and only in the hopes that it could encourage others. Prior to the dream, I had been praying that God opens my eyes to all that He wanted me to do and that I would share whatever He wanted me to share upon His prompting, unapologetically. I admit that I really got a kick out of this one. I grinned with delight when I found out what the words I had heard spoken in my dream meant. I believe He has an amazing sense of humor. I'd also like to admit that I was slightly bummed that the message wasn't more spectacular. I mean seriously, Lord? Everyone already knows you want them to follow You; that is nothing new. The message was short and simplistically sweet, and it's often the way I hear from Him. You can't misunderstand or misinterpret its meaning. In my spirit, I felt that I needed to continue to simply follow Him and stay in His Word.

At the end of certain dreams, I may hear someone shout at me or say a word that I'm to remember when I wake up. One dream ended in just such a way, with the name "Gideon" echoing in my mind. I usually sort of say, "Okay, Lord, I get it," when I hear it, then follow through with research regarding the name and scripture first thing in the morning. It had been ages since I had read about or studied Gideon. I was astonished and almost brought to tears at how each scripture read pertained to something relevant in my life or the country at exactly the time of my dream. As the day went on and I was listening to a pastor on social media, he was also talking about Gideon, of all people. Those kinds of moments, I believe, are little winks from God letting us know that we are on the right track and encouraging us to keep going. It is in those exact times that you feel the genuine love of the Father and become so appreciative that He loves you enough to send little winks your way. The winks or blessings often appear when we least expect them to but are always right on time.

Our dreams can also deliver a warning to help us prepare for an event that is about to happen or could possibly occur in the not-too-distant future. Another dream from quite a while ago exemplified that exact possibility. In the dream, I learned that this particular person would become pregnant. She seemed incredibly bubbly and happy all the while throughout the dream. I was but a shadow to her. She acted as if I didn't exist. I did hear her say that the name of the baby girl would be "Sorrow." It was almost as if I was a spectator to all that was unfolding before me. When I woke up, the dream was still so vivid to me. Parts of it made me overjoyed, and other parts made me sad, and I couldn't figure out why. Fast forward a few days later, and I mentioned to this person that she was in my dream and had a baby girl, but I didn't share any other part of the dream. Another week or so went by, and it was learned that she was expecting. It pains me to tell you the rest of the story. She was pregnant and ended up miscarrying after only a few months. My heart was aching for her as I remembered the name I was given of the baby in the dream. I'm thankful I never shared that part with her, as her pain in losing her child was already insurmountable. But the name wasn't pertinent to the actual name of the baby; the dream was for me. Since the dream and unfolding of her life events, our relationship changed. Sometimes, we are not meant to share a dream with others. We need to be able to discern if a dream is simply a way for God to prepare us for what is to come so that we know how to pray properly. A dream could also be His way of uncovering sin, shortcomings, or a way of teaching us valuable lessons pertaining to our own lives.

Yet another dream, I was told by a stranger to "remember your twos and threes" right before waking up. That's basically all I could recall from the dream. I'll sometimes say a little prayer that if I'm to remember anything, that God will bring it back to my mind when appropriate, and if it's nonsense or not from Him, that it will fade away. Well, it didn't fade. For days and days and days, I was getting the numbers two and three in strange places. Dreams can have symbols recurring in them, and numbers are symbols that often have meaning. I enjoyed trying to figure out what those specific numbers meant. Could it be my friend's or niece's birthday? Was something significant going to happen then? Was it a special year that something major would occur world or country-wide? So, I entered it in my journal, dated it, and tucked it away with that same old let's just wait and see mentality. The numbers wouldn't go away and became extremely annoying. After saying a prayer, I told the Lord I'd just go through some random scripture that had those numbers in it, expecting Him to just show me what He wanted me to see. Imagine how baby Christians just open the Bible and point to a scripture that fits exactly what they are going through at the time in their new walk with the Lord. I approached the task with the same mentality. I should have known better. I think I started in the New Testament, and something strange began to happen. I developed a hunger for more and more of the Word, which had been a little prayer of mine, months before the dream. I went through almost every book of the Bible, remembering my twos and threes, and wrote them all down on a legal pad. It was therapy. It was good medicine. He knew what I really needed more than I knew myself. Sweet. Simplistic and pure. That's the way He deals with me. In the gentlest of ways so that I don't mistake the master in the message. I don't always get it right and have spent many years going around the same mountain before I finally learned the lessons He was sending my way. I do still dream. He still gives me coded messages in my dreams from time to time. That doesn't make me an expert in the field by any stretch of the imagination. I'm just one of those supernaturally dysfunctional crackpots that have been around since history began. I love to learn and completely understand that the more I learn, the less I truly know. Especially when it comes to the things of God, He can use any one of us in amazing and miraculous ways if we tune in to Him and listen to what He's trying to tell us or even show us. "For God does not show favoritism" (Romans 2:11). What He does for one of us, He will do for any of us since He loves us all the same. That is a very soothing thought.

If God can use our dream life to communicate or edify us in a positive and healthy way, it would be probable that the devil would also try to invade our dream state to wreak havoc or any kind of negative reaction as well. It is best to always test the spirit, as explained to us in 1 John 4, when it comes to anxious dreams or messages that target us at any given time. If we don't receive a quick meaning from a disturbing dream, it would be advantageous to forget it, as it could most likely be sent from the enemy. Remember that God is not the author of confusion; the devil is, according to 1 Corinthians 14:33.

It is interesting to note that we are living during a season when prophets, several self-proclaimed, are coming out of the woodwork on social media professing God's message to all the world or to whoever will listen to them. It is only my opinion that on several occasions, these declarations have become somewhat of a slippery slope for Christians, especially those living in our country. We have been continually bombarded with negative stories and blatant lies from the media, an establishment that we once held dear, relied on, and wholeheartedly believed in without question. Some prophets are speaking out against these specific outlets in ways that bring genuine hope and encouragement to the people in our country who grow weary of their bias. A few prophets have been spewing continual doom and gloom as well. Some scared Americans, including Christians, have gone so far as to sell all their belongings, quit jobs, and have moved their families to other states or countries in order to protect themselves from the obvious catastrophic devastation they believe to soon be coming to our nation. People have been hoarding food, toilet paper (had to mention toilet paper), gas, guns, ammunition and have been preparing for the impending apocalyptic end of the world. Some have gone so far as to not listen to the news at all but only listen to the latest prophecy, and believe me, there are many that are posted every single day. It is extremely important to note at this point that if we put prophecy first, listening to it more than we read the Bible or spend time with God, we are opening another unwanted, supernaturally dysfunctional door to the devil. More precisely, we are opening ourselves up to an invasion by familiar spirits. Familiar spirits, as you may recall, are under the complete control of their master, Satan. It is their goal to manipulate, spread lies, deception, and confuse people to keep them from God's plans and promises. As we are told in 1 Thessalonians 5:21, "Test everything. Hold on to the good." That is exactly what we need to do where the prophetic is concerned. Some prophets are truly speaking from the Lord, but others may not be. Testing everything is the only way to keep your heart protected during this extremely challenging era we are living in.

I would suggest that you draw nearer to the Lord during these disturbing and unsettling times if that's what your heart truly desires. If you go to Him with your longing to hear from Him, follow His promptings and learn of His ways, He is faithful and will show up in surprising and unexpected ways. As we are told in Jeremiah 33:3, "Call to me and I will answer you and tell you great and unsearchable things you do not know." Soaking in His presence until He shows up often yields an overwhelming sense of peace as you rest in the warm embrace of His love. He loves us through encouragement and gives us a renewed purpose and unrelenting desire for more of Him. He strengthens our innermost being, renews our youth, as the eagles (Psalm 103:5), and energizes our physical body to be able to complete the tasks He sets before us. I don't know about you, but I cannot physically or mentally get through a single day on this planet without His mercy or endless grace and compassion. He is the source of my hope. He can be yours too.

12

When God Whispers

Do you ever wonder why it is that so many individuals today proclaim to hear from God practically on a daily basis? Thanks to the ever-evolving world of social media, we can get these seemingly supernaturally charged messages from these folks anywhere or at any time on our phones, computers, or televisions. Does it seem odd to you that God is downloading messages to only a select few while the rest of us walk around dazed, spiritually wounded, and wondering if God even hears us when we pray? What is so special about them, anyway? Why does He only speak to them, and why do they seem to know exactly what He is doing or what we all as Christians should be doing with our lives? Well, my friend, if you've had similar questions, you are definitely not alone.

Some people are wired or specifically designed as an antenna for supernatural downloads from the Almighty, as crazy as it may sound. There could be bloodline blessings that can give some a bit of an advantage as far as actually hearing from the Lord more easily than others. Their upline could include pastors, popes, kings, or just simply Bible-praying ancestors who continually blessed and prayed over their families. This type of ancestral upline may usher in a positive and functional supernatural probability of easily tuning in to God's frequency.

Those who have bloodline curses and are notoriously supernaturally dysfunctional could be wired a tad bit differently. It doesn't mean that they can't hear from God themselves, but it could mean a multitude of evil intending minions make it their mission to do everything within their power to keep the Lord's messages from getting through. If such messages do get through to their intended vessel, these low-level devils will then work overtime to make one believe the message to be false or that he or she is not worthy enough to hear from our heavenly Father. All lies, of course, but easy enough to believe when you find yourself struggling in the moment.

Some well-meaning and highly regarded Christian leaders, appearing to have it all together, give us downloads supposedly from heaven itself, making it look so easy. They seem to have practically perfect lives, filled to overflowing with God's biggest, brightest, and best blessings. I don't know about you, but I sometimes have an extremely difficult time believing their sincerity. Through years of striving to perfect my own faith walk, I would often find myself comparing my life with those types of leaders or speakers. Unfortunately, predisposed and wired for depression due to my familial bloodline, this type of comparison often brought about despair, discouragement, and unhealthy thoughts about God's love or plans for me. You've read enough to know that this is obviously another trap from the enemy. Becoming self-absorbed or discouraged are many times numbers one and two on the devil's greatest hits list. If he can get us discouraged, our entire spirit and attitude may fall, and other deeper deceptions could begin to work as well.

So, are these leaders always hearing from God directly? If they are, why can't I receive their timely messages? For me personally, the message gets blocked because I simply can't relate to them. Perhaps they haven't gone through enough challenges in their own lives, sharing the ups and downs of how God helped them to overcome their personal hardships. Their lack of challenging life experiences has led me to believe they may not even know what they are talking about and haven't earned the right to tell me how I should be living. I gravitate towards people who have been in the trenches. Those who had lost all hope, were real with God about unimaginable losses and tragedy, or felt themselves sinking in their own selfish sin. The point is if you have never had to go through any type of trial in your life, and you are trying to pastor or lead me, I'm most likely not going to be able to listen to you. Fair enough?

I believe that many of the challenges we face and ultimately overcome occur in order for us to have the tools necessary to help others get over or get through similar setbacks. It fills us with compassion for all they have had to endure since we have already been there ourselves. We know such attacks are from the enemy, but God can turn those messes into our message so that we can be a blessing and encouragement to someone else.

As you can imagine, I grew up with a lot of personal hang-ups. I mean, you name it, I either did it, believed it, or felt I had to hide all my imperfections so that others would approve of me; what an exhausting way to live. By the time I was in college, I had my guard up high and acted as though I had my act together, with an emphasis on the acting part. One specific day in my psychology class, we had to go around the room and share a way that we felt inferior or discriminated against. In this class, participation was part of the grade, so there was absolutely no pressure at all. Yes, that last part was mentioned with a slightly sarcastic tone. I was a somewhat quiet, private student and didn't like to speak in public. As people began to share, nothing really came into my mind at first, and I began to panic. Should I tell them about the fact that my real dad didn't want me? Or perhaps I should share that I had to wear super thick glasses that magnified my eyes until I was sixteen years old, making me look like a bug? Maybe I should tell them about how I was a tomboy growing up and always felt ugly and unwanted? Dare I share about how my brothers' friends never even knew I was their little sister? No, if I shared anything personal, it would show my true weakness or make others find out who I really was underneath the superficial daily fun-loving act. So, when it was my turn to speak, I lied and told my favorite professor and the entire class that I was discriminated against and thought to be dumb entirely due to my blonde hair color. I could see my professor wasn't buying my lame attempt at just getting through the class. I felt so bad afterward and wanted so much to go in and privately tell my professor how sorry I was, etcetera, but never did.

The point of the above story was that the act of being perfect, seeming to have it all together, and hiding any and all weakness most definitely made me unrelatable. I missed out on being a participant in a pure discussion, a possible moment of healing and understanding, or even a new friendship. I would have received a far better grade for the day if I had shared what was really on my heart. God was whispering even then, but I wasn't listening.

The negative self-image I had cocooned myself in while growing up left lasting baggage that took decades to unpack and leave behind. Yes, I was the epitome of just plain old dysfunction on steroids. And that was on my best day. If you consider the supernatural bloodline curse that perversely and continually hovers over me and my clan, you can imagine the twists and turns my life has consistently taken since my initial entry onto the planet. I have had to chip away at my own cocoon of depression, armed to the teeth with Scripture and declarations galore. There have been days, battle-weary and just too tired to care, that I have felt utterly alone in my quest to become healthy and pliable enough to complete the quest the Lord has had me on. Those days sometimes yielded the biggest, brightest, and tastiest fruit of all, especially the ones where God showed up and gently whispered in my direction.

The time that my family lived in Tennessee was an exceptionally lonely and soul-searching one for me. The hubby was busy with his job and new position with his company. My older three kids were teenagers, busy with school and sports. This left me at home with our little toddler. There are so many times in my life that I pause and just thank God for bringing our little love into the world, and our stint in Tennessee was one of them. She kept me occupied with many fun and lighthearted moments. God knew what He was doing. No surprise there.

Tennessee is where the idea of this book was birthed through lots of soul-searching, heartaches, doubts, and fears. An interesting thing began to happen. I felt a growing heaviness settle in on me, and I just couldn't seem to overcome it. It didn't matter what I did; it wouldn't go away. Depression? Absolutely. I was in a beautiful home with a healthy and amazing family, affluent neighborhood, and lovely state with endless fun things to do. And I was miserable. Lonely. I am telling you it is extremely possible to live in a home full of children with a loving husband and still feel lonely and close to a breakdown of epic proportions. I knew I had no reason to be feeling the way I did and wanted to uncover its origin and end it once and for all if I could.

During this time, I had also developed an unquenchable desire to find out how and why my biological father could give away his baby girl. I would often look at my children and think, "I don't ever want to miss a moment of their growing up." I could never leave them and could never even imagine my life without them in it. It tugs at the heartstrings in the knowledge that my very own father not only didn't want me but asked my new stepfather to officially adopt me. Up until that time, I didn't realize how much his abandonment had truly affected me. I wanted to know why and set out to find him and ask him myself, which is exactly what I did.

It didn't take long for me to discover his location. I finally agreed to a phone call and, through tears, asked him what I wanted to know. He explained that upon his return from the Vietnam War, he suffered from post-traumatic stress syndrome and couldn't take care of himself or anyone else. The war had taken its toll on him, that much I totally understood. He also mentioned that as I got older, he would often watch me, from across the street, as I walked into the school building, just to get a glimpse of me. In his own way, I am sure he loved me and probably still does to this day. I did somewhat begin to understand him and his reasoning from those conversations. Again, God knew what He was doing. My life would have turned out very differently had I grown up with him as my father. I felt a little sorry for him, exchanged some correspondence, and even sent him a scrapbook of myself and my children. Then I cut all ties permanently. I received the answers I needed to move on. The father who raised me truly loved me as if I was his own flesh and blood. There is no way that I would risk hurting my parent's feelings, even slightly, by having an ongoing relationship with my biological father.

Though I was feeling a little lighter in spirit, there was still a gnawing and lonely persistent feeling that I couldn't seem to shake. I tearfully went to the Lord on several occasions asking for healing and help. I continually wondered what was wrong with me and why did He seem so distant? In the meantime, memories began to flood my mind. All those feelings of being an ugly little girl with brothers who didn't love her back, paternal relatives who barely acknowledged her existence, and never feeling good enough to deserve to succeed in life, came flooding back in excruciatingly painful and unrelenting ways. Would I ever be happy again?

Though I did sense it at the time, there were supernatural influences continually shooting fiery darts at every turn. I was already predisposed to majorly dysfunctional tendencies. These depression-inducing tactics of the enemy were obviously trying to seal the deal and halt any destiny the Lord had in mind for me. Though I hadn't lost my faith completely, it had indeed shrunk to the size of a mustard seed. In a final act of humble surrender, or perhaps more accurately, a slightly sarcastic or angry act of surrender, I laid it all down at the feet of Jesus. I basically told Him that it was all in His hands, my faith, my depression, and my happiness. From that moment on, I'd quit asking for His help in getting out from under this oppression and just carry on the best that I could.

Not long after my surrender, while preparing dinner, a sweet spirit washed over me, stopping me in my tracks. A voice clearly whispered, "You are not that abandoned little girl anymore." Just like that, I knew God had taken the time to answer my prayer with a whisper. Happy tears formed in my eyes as I let out a laugh and thanked Him for speaking life back into me again. The heaviness had instantly lifted, and a peaceful, joyful feeling replaced it. I was healed of past hurts, insecurities, and disappointments at that exact moment. I was free, and I knew it was for good.

I do believe that God speaks to us more often than we realize. Some proudly proclaim that they hear His audible voice almost every day. I have no way of knowing if their accounts are accurate, if they are really hearing from God, if they are being deceived, or if they are doing so only for a deep-seated need for attention. I know that God can do whatever He wants and talk to whoever He wants, whenever He wants. He is God, after all.

In that kitchen, years ago, I heard a quiet whisper, but not a loud voice. I knew it was from God. He had met me where I was and lovingly answered my prayer. Though I greatly desire to hear God's voice every day, He seldom speaks to me in an unmistakably loud way. In fact, I've only ever heard His voice audibly one time in my life so far. I sincerely hope it won't be the last.

Several years ago, I had a breast biopsy taken while we were living in Michigan. I had family praying for me and had faith that God would see me through, whatever the outcome would be. For some reason, I drove to the doctor's office by myself to finally receive the results. My husband was at work, and I most likely had told him not to take time off for my appointment. Upon arrival, I just sat in my car, hands on the steering wheel with my head down as silent tears began to fall. No prayer, just quiet sobs as I tried to pull myself together enough to go in and hear my results. It was at that exact moment when I heard God say, "I got this." By the way, this was right before the big "I Got This...God" signs were popular and appearing everywhere. At that point in time, I audibly heard His voice. His undeniable peace washed over me as warmth rose from my feet to my face. I knew I was ready to receive my results from the doctor, which just happened to be benign. He didn't lie. He had my back, so to speak, and all was fine.

These moments are being shared to show that God whispers and speaks to us in many ways throughout our lives and desires that we simply take the time to listen. I don't believe that He speaks to everyone in exactly the same manner because we are all so different in nature and spiritual makeup. Besides, God loves variety and takes pleasure in surprising us with His presence.

Several years later, I was in a car accident. A red truck had blocked my view of an on-coming car that I ended up hitting directly on its passenger side while it was turning in front of me. Gripping the steering wheel and slightly in a state of shock, OnStar began telling me that help was on the way. Around that time, a woman came running out of a building, yelling at me to get out of the car, as gas appeared to be leaking underneath it. No one was hurt, just a few minor bruises and slight fractures. That was the first miracle, as the engine had moved entirely off its block and could have easily landed in my lap or at least pinned me in my seat. I remember that during a split second of the accident, I felt as though two large hands were holding me in place, one on my belly and one on my back, preventing any movement. Though the airbags went off, they never touched me. Once again, God showed up, but this time, without uttering a word to me. I'm not even saying that those were His hands exactly holding me in place, though I wholeheartedly believe He sent a heavenly helper in my direction that morning. I never heard an audible voice or whisper, but my heart felt His gentle squeeze and a knowing that it was from Him. That was no coincidence.

The accident reminds me of a line in a favorite older contemporary Christian song when the singer sang, "Near misses all around me, accidents unknown, though, I never see with human eyes the hands that lead me home." Undoubtedly, I could not see in the natural giant hands holding me in place during my accident, but in the supernatural, I believed that they were there. Likewise, in your own life, you may never know all your "near misses" that God had a hand in for your protection. I do not believe in coincidences, but rather in supernatural forces either trying to protect and help us along life's journey or those designed to try to wipe us out. As the song goes, they are always all around us, and if your angels are anything like mine, they are probably working overtime to help you accomplish all that God desires for you to do during your earthly stay.

God promised in His Word that He would never leave you nor forsake you (Deuteronomy 31:6). He is always with us. Is it so hard to believe that He speaks to us, whispers in our hearts, or graces us with a knowing in our spirit whenever He senses that we desperately need to hear from Him? It's not difficult at all when you remember that, first and foremost, He is love. He loves us all individually, passionately, and unconditionally. Sometimes He is just waiting for us to slow down, be still and listen. He is patiently standing by, hoping that we seek His face in our quiet moments, inviting His lovingkindness to enter the room. Instead of just praying and getting up immediately following your "amen" to go about the busyness of your day, stay awhile following your prayer to see if He wishes to reveal anything to you. Sometimes, we rush off too quickly after our list of prayer wishes and quench His spirit, ultimately missing a great blessing. The greatest of blessings or end goal of any prayer should be a desire to bask in His presence and just love on our heavenly Father. He deserves it, He inhabits it, and He delights Himself in it. Simply stated, He loves you and wants to spend time with you. Besides all of that, He is extremely easy to love.

13

Wholehearted

I couldn't let this book conclude without first mentioning a truly amazing family, epitomizing the steadfast and uncompromising belief of God's love for His children. What makes their story even more incredible is their uncanny ability to lean on and into the Lord in the wake of tremendous tragedy without losing their faith. Even though they were experiencing their own grief at the time, they managed to be a continual source of encouragement to those around them. I'm humbled beyond words by their example of God's grace and blessed to be able to call them my family.

Several years ago, on Valentine's Day, our family suffered an incredible and shocking loss. My cousin, Elizabeth, died unexpectedly in the early morning as she was, we believe, going about her usual routine of making the morning coffee. There were no warning signs upon her rising that those were to be her last moments here on the earth. Her husband and three children were already off to work and school, respectively. She was the second daughter that my aunt and uncle had lost and the second sister my cousin, Janey, had to say goodbye to.

How quickly all their lives had been forever changed in the blink of an eye. The ache in their souls and the cries in their hearts had to be deafening that Valentine's Day and, in the days, to follow as we all struggled for understanding. Death truly does leave a hole in our hearts. There are no words that can comfort such a great loss, the loss of a child. As a mother myself, I can't even begin to understand the loss of not only one but two children. It doesn't follow the natural order of things in our mortal and limited minds. It is normal to seek understanding and to ask God how He could allow such a thing to occur. Especially when my aunt and uncle were always unwavering in their faith and love for the Lord, following in all His ways. They are an amazing Christian family, full of hope and love, who continually lighten up any room they enter. They exemplify God's love for us as they unashamedly declare His grace and glory to those around them.

The truth is that no one knows why bad or unspeakable things happen to good people. Ministers are trained to tell us that it is because we live in a fallen world. Well, that is true enough. But it certainly doesn't lend much help in the mending of a broken or wounded heart.

I began to ponder the "why" of my cousin's untimely and tragic death while simultaneously thinking about how short our life on this planet truly is in comparison to eternity. An old song quickly crept into my mind describing the feeling of being hole-hearted. Somewhat appropriate that it came to me that Valentine's Day when Elizabeth left this earth. One line in the song stated, "If I'm not blind, why can't I see that a circle can't fit where a square should be." Don't we all feel that way at certain times in our own lives? If I'm not blind, why can't I see or understand the reason certain events unfold the way they do? Why can't I see the meaning in all that my aunt and uncle have had to deal with or any of the tragedies we've each had to face? On many occasions in my own life, I have found myself humming this song and relating to its lyrics.

The chorus goes on to state that the hole in the singer's heart can only be filled by the receiver of its lyrics or the precise individual the song is about. Though a secular song, I can't help but relate it to our own individual walk of faith.

There is purposefully a spiritual or supernatural hole in our hearts that we are all individually born with. It is my belief that we spend our lives trying to fill it up with love, relationships, religion, careers, trips, material things, or social media, etcetera. We try to fill this empty part of ourselves with one thing, maybe even to the extreme, only to have that very thing taken away from us. Or perhaps the very thing we have chosen to focus on or fulfill us has become all-consuming to the point of risking our health and, most likely, our happiness. Maybe the thing with which we've chosen to fill that void or hole with may eventually cost us our very soul. Or maybe we ultimately become disillusioned with our hole-filler and end up feeling discouraged, disappointed, hopeless, or even forgotten.

In my opinion, God is the only one who can fill up this hole in our lives. If I have faith in nothing, there is no hope, and I lose myself. God fills me up with His love and hope every single day of my life. Though I will never understand why I've had to go through some challenging times or why the people I love have had unthinkable tragedies happen to them, I will rely totally on my heavenly Father, who loves us all the same, to see me through. Just as my aunt and uncle have done through the heart-wrenching deaths of their daughters and my cousin Janey's loss of both of her sisters, they have remained steadfast and unwavering in their faith and love for the Lord. Though it is undoubtedly impossible to ever get over such tragic losses, God is always there to aid in the healing and see us through. God desires to heal the wounded soul. He wants us to be "wholehearted," lacking no good thing (Psalm 34:10).

In our loneliest and darkest hours, the Lord desires to remind us, "...Never will I leave you; never will I forsake you" (Hebrews 13:5). Though admittedly, sometimes, when we are in the deepest of trenches, we may not always feel God's presence physically. It may be difficult to understand how we can desperately need His touch, yet at the same time feel totally abandoned, as if He is nowhere to be found. It is so easy to stay in the pit of loneliness, feeling His distance to mean that He's far out of our reach and may not care enough to hold us close to His heart. Though it is common to feel that God has left us to grieve alone, we know that we can never go by or even trust our feelings. We always go by what we know, and we know that His Word is true. In Numbers 23:19, it is written, "God is not human, that he should lie, not a human being, that he should change his mind. Does he speak and then not act? Does he promise and not fulfill?" God said it; then it's truth. Even though He may seem distant at certain times in our lives, He has told us that He will never leave us, regardless of how we feel. As challenging as it may be at times, we try to take comfort in the fact that He is always with us.

I do not believe that my family's predisposition to supernatural bloodline curses to be the blame for my aunt and uncle's tragic losses of two out of their three daughters. I do, however, believe that when a family or individual breaks bloodline curses by serving and loving the Lord, the devil and his demons often work overtime to cause as much misery and torment as they possibly can. I don't believe it to be God's will that lives are lost unexpectedly, but I know Him to lovingly pick up and repair the pieces of broken hearts from those left behind when the unspeakable does occur. In the case of my family, the enemy's schemes failed miserably. My incredible aunt, uncle, and cousin, Janey, love the Lord and continue to lean on Him daily. Their faith has never been stronger. They are the epitome of supernatural functionality at their best and know full well the true secret of living the "wholehearted" life.

14

The Waiting

To quote one of my favorite singers, "You take it on faith, you take it to the heart, the waiting is hardest part."[6] Truer words were never spoken. Though patience is thought to be a desired virtue, waiting has never been my forte. Full disclosure, I'm still working on this particular trait and get plenty of opportunities to try to perfect it. I am still convinced that God's timing is always best, but why does it have to take so earthly long for desired results or answers to manifest themselves?

All kidding aside, there can be unprecedented potential for personal growth and supernatural enlightenment when perfecting the art of waiting on the Lord. In Isaiah 40:31 (KJV), we are told, "But they that wait upon the Lord shall renew their strength; they shall mount up with wings as eagles; they shall run and not be weary; and they shall walk, and not faint." I learned this scripture as a song when I was a little girl and would emphasize the ending words we sang, "Teach me, Lord, teach

---
6 Tom Petty, "The Waiting"

me Lord to wait." Amen to that one. This scripture reminds us that, though it may be the hardest thing to do, we all still have to do it. It's how we behave in the waiting that's most important.

It is no secret that we live in a fast-paced world that cultivates instant gratification on whatever whim we're feeling at the moment. We can get whatever we want right away, or dependent upon your Amazon membership, within a couple of days or so. We have fast food, fast transportation, the ability to watch a movie on our phone within minutes, can send correspondence or text messages instantly, post videos on social media with the push of a button, and use credit cards to buy something before we can truly afford it. We get irritated or feel slighted if we must wait in a line for longer than five minutes, unless, of course, it's for Starbucks. Our entire current culture seems to have lost the art of waiting.

As the unfortunate COVID-19 stopped the world in its tracks, humankind was thrown into months, over a year so far, into a holding pattern. Many of us have been fearfully confined to our homes, separated from loved ones, desperately praying for its end. Though we know God hears our prayers and cries for protection or for the end of this virus crisis, its devastation defiantly continues. Why hasn't He answered our prayers, and what are we supposed to do while we wait?

Perhaps it's not the pandemic and closing of the world that has caused the endless feeling of waiting, with no glimpse of its ending, in your own life. Maybe you've been praying for months or years for a healing that hasn't come, though you've remained vigilant in your faith and steadfast in your prayer life. The list could go on and on of the challenges you've been praying for, whether financial, physical, spiritual, or even for the salvation of loved ones. God seems distant, though you know He's there, and you wonder what He's waiting for or even perhaps what you have done wrong to hasten the end of your own personal holding pattern. The disappointments come at us full force, as our country and the world seem to continue to freefall into a state of stupor, indifference, or just plain intolerance.

Depressed yet? You've made it this far through the book, and if you can indulge me for a little while longer, we'll try to dissect the why of the wait. It is my hope that we may also be able to uncover our mission during the waiting period as well as ways to remain uplifted and useful to God's plans and purpose for our lives.

Negativity begets negativity, and misery loves company. Have you ever noticed that at certain points in your day, especially during crisis mode, your spirit feels heavy, and your physical body may even begin to show signs of exhaustion? During those specific moments, have you ever phoned a friend or family member and unleashed all the negativity you were feeling during that time? Do you recall how you felt by the end of the conversation? Unless you spoke with someone who is always a little ray of sunshine that somehow lifted you out of the negative funk you were in, you most likely felt worse upon the ending of the conversation. Not only that, but now that you spewed your own negativity to your friend, you've most likely brought his or her spirit down a notch or two as well. The negativity, in turn, may then have a chance to grow and spread.

I have personally done this very thing. At the end of the conversation, I always felt worse, as if I were Eeyore with a dark, gloomy cloud hanging over my head. I never felt better. I did exactly as the enemy wished at that point in time. I sowed supernaturally major dysfunction in speaking out negative words to my friend, being that little ball of happiness that I was at the time, ruined her day, and ultimately reaped what I had sown, allowing the darkness to fester and grow within myself. I couldn't blame the Holy Spirit at all for hitting the road or being silent. I played right into the enemy's plans, and what's even sadder is that I knew better.

When moments like that occur, by complaining, whining, or spreading negativity, I ultimately made it impossible for the Lord to bless me at all. There is no way that any prayer of deliverance could be answered, as it wouldn't even be able to break through the supernatural barrier my negativity built between the Lord and myself. Consequently, this type of behavior inevitably prolonged my waiting period. It doesn't take a genius to realize that what I had been doing wasn't working, and it was making me miserable. The negativity got so bad at times that I didn't even want to be around myself. Ever been there? Well, take heart, dear one. There is hope for us yet!

Though the waiting period experienced could, in fact, stem from our very own supernatural dysfunction, as indicated from my personal example, it's not always the primary reason for it. I can't pretend to know the Father's heart as to the why of your wait, especially since He deals with each one of us differently. I can, however, share with you a few things I've learned along the way in the hope that you find a little peace and comfort in the middle of yours.

Comparing ourselves to others may sicken your soul, hinder your spiritual walk, and inhibit your faith. It often seems that when we are in the thick of it, bringing our petitions to God and praying our little hearts out, that along comes a friend or family member who seems to get all their prayers answered quickly. It's as if they have God on speed-dial, and He's just waiting to give them all they ask for. Not only that, but they just can't wait to share all that He has done for them while you get to listen and enthusiastically cheer them on. Afterward, you may need a slight heart check or at least some time to repent of that green-eyed monster you've allowed to stealthily creep back into your life. It must be obvious to you as well that this, too, in fact, is part of the testing. Can we be genuinely happy for others who have been blessed by the Lord and have steadily received answers to their prayers while we have been waiting for years to receive our own? Yes, there have been times in my life when I've had to use the old "fake it 'til you make it" mentality and act as though their breakthroughs meant more to me than anything else in the world. Following this type of exchange usually provoked an episode of intense sighs, grumblings under my breath, and concluded with a major complaint list directly targeted to heaven. For the record, I don't recommend such behavior. Besides, who are we trying to fool anyway? God absolutely always knows what's truly in our hearts. He knows the good, the bad, and the ugly. We may as well admit our true feelings, ask for forgiveness and, if you are anything like me, ask for an attitude adjustment, just to have all bases covered.

I have heard some well-meaning biblical teachers state that God answers all prayer. They often end such statements by explaining to us that His answers are usually "yes, no, or wait." I'm not sure I'm altogether thrilled with any of those responses, if I'm being completely honest. We all desire for God to answer our requests with a "yes, let's do this, kiddo." I could easily get behind a lifetime of quickly answered "yes" prayers, and I'm sure you could too. Though, if we think about it, a lifetime of yesses, without much effort involved in their attainment, may result in a bunch of self-centered toddler-minded adults. Nobody's got time for that type of scenario. The second and third answers I could totally do without, however, as they may bring about or prolong uncomfortable challenges. Besides all of that, we've already established that we, as human beings, do not like to wait.

Another well-known pastor often exclaims, with extreme pleasure, that God answers all his prayers and never tells him no. Although difficult to hide the slight annoyance felt with that last pastor's comment, I sincerely appreciate his enthusiasm and wish I could claim the same. He just may be on to something, as it says in the Bible that God's promises are always "Yes and Amen" (2 Corinthians 1:20). I have heard this pastor recite that very scripture countless times as if it were air to him. I wonder, if I start declaring the same scripture over my own prayer requests, will God quickly do the same for me? Well, unfortunately, I haven't found that to be exactly the way God wishes to operate in my personal journey. It is not God's design for us to come to Him with our Santa Claus list of prayer requests, expecting them all to be delivered exactly in the way we desire. He loves us far too much for that.

And so, we wait.

We wait, and we pray without ceasing for the answers to manifest and become our reality. We wait and hold on to our faith that the one who knows us best loves us most and will never ever leave us. We pray when God seems distant and remind ourselves that we can never go by our soulish feelings. We cling to every scripture we can find pertaining to our specific need or crisis and declare them over our lives.

The Bible is our guidebook. It's the living word of God, and His word is true. He's given us a special book of wisdom to all of life's answers, yet we barely take the time to dust it off and peruse its pages. His promises are free and ours for the claiming. Yes, pastor, I agree that all of God's answers to our prayers are, indeed, "yes and amen." It says as much in the Bible, so it has to be true in the right context.

For argument's sake, let's say that we get on this crazy claim-your-promises-to answered-prayer train and apply it to our daily lives, yet the responses from the Almighty still fail to present themselves. What then? You guessed it. We patiently wait because we know He is faithful.

No, it isn't easy, it isn't comfortable, and it most certainly isn't fun. I can tell you first-hand, as one who has been waiting, praying, and expecting divine healing for almost nine years now as this book goes to print. It's been a long and often frustrating journey, as well as a continually painful battle. I have, at times, lost my faith, almost completely given up, and even sort of yelled at God a time or two. I certainly questioned Him on more than one occasion. All the while, He was continually working on my faith and, every so often, even sent a little wink my way.

I finally got really good at waiting. Not only did I get good at it, but I also actually learned a lot about myself along the way. As you can imagine, knowing my history as you now do, I had a lot of negative issues that needed dealing with, toot sweet! You can pathetically cry out to God for only so long until your tear ducts dry up, your face swells, your nose runs, and your eyes get too puffy to clearly see when you finally come to the end of yourself and decide that enough is enough. I finally fell at the feet of Jesus and told Him, once and for all, that though I still believed His will was to heal me, I wasn't going to keep asking Him for healing. I switched instead to thanking Him that it already happened. I do the same to this very day.

I'm the type of person who always must find the answer to a problem and know the why behind the question. I used to try to understand and dissect the reason I still wasn't healed or why some prayers had yet to be answered. After all, we know that God can just breathe in our direction and heal us or send a blessing our way. I used to continually wonder what I was doing wrong. Did I have some buried sin I had yet to confess, or was my faith simply not strong enough? I just couldn't seem to figure out why others received answers from the Lord in a timely fashion, while I spent years believing and received none.

When the pain becomes unbearable, whether physical, spiritual, or even mental, the enemy puts doubt in your mind. He's predictable and consistent in that regard. When you are at your weakest, he will go in for the kill shot and hope to get you out of your faith, into the flesh, and ultimately, try to make you lose all faith in God's ability to heal or get you through your challenges. I am no exception, as I'm already supernaturally predisposed to the mother-load of dysfunction with a bloodline of successfully curse-laden outcomes. We also know that the devil often tips his hand during such attacks, showing us his true intent. This gives us our edge as we then know what to come against, bind, and pray for. His tricks are nothing new, as he's been using the same tactics since the fall of Adam.

During a particularly painful and low point in my faith walk, the attacks ferociously followed, one right after another, until all I could do was say the name above all names, "Jesus." I couldn't even pray. I had absolutely nothing left. I had no will to fight it and no prayer to send since I had already prayed to the point of spiritual exhaustion. With the tears rolling down my face, I silently cried out his name in an act of complete surrender. Then the thought came to me, though I believe it to have been downloaded from the Lord Himself, "If you never know the why, will you still love Me?" As I truly paused and considered the question, the answer from my hole-filled yet aching heart was, "Yes, Lord. Of course, I will." At that moment, something shifted in my soul, and I knew that no matter what, "God's got this," as the saying goes. I also realized that I may never understand why I've spent years in a holding pattern, waiting on my miracle or answered prayers, but that it really was okay. I honestly didn't have to know the reason. I would always praise Him in the storm and believe that He will always see me through it.

Isaiah 43:2 explains, "When you pass through the waters, I will be with you." He goes on to tell us that the rivers won't overtake us and that the fire will not be able to burn us because He's always with us. Whether we feel His presence or not. He will never leave us, nor forsake us (Hebrews 13:5). As He stated in Isaiah 43, He has promised to be with us in the storm as we pass through the waters. We can find peace in his promises because we know His words are always true.

Though we may never know the why of our waiting, we can trust that the one who knows us best and loves us most has it all under control and will see us through. That really is true faith, isn't it? Faith is believing, especially when we can't see the desired outcome. Though we may get heavenly glimpses from time to time, we don't always see the Lord in the natural, and yet still believe. Prayer is our superpower, but faith is our anchor.

There is an amazing freedom in the act of letting go of the need to know the why of things or happenings in the world. To just simply "Trust in the Lord with all your heart and lean not on your own understanding" (Proverbs 3:5) is a beautiful way to live. The rest of that verse tells us that He will ultimately direct our paths and basically help us with our God-given destination and purpose. I pray that you find some comfort in that particular knowledge going forward and facing all obstacles placed in your path.

A final word to the wise while you're in the waiting stage of unanswered prayer, please learn from my mistakes. It is practically impossible to get through it all while maintaining a bad attitude. I mean, you may eventually get through to the manifestation of your miracle, but it will take you a lot longer than you'd like. God's timing is not our own, but it's always best. Besides, there are lessons to be learned in the waiting, and believe it or not, many God-winks and baby blessings along the journey. I don't want you to miss out on those. They fuel our faith. They are God's way of saying to us, "It's okay, keep going. I got you." It's the way we wait that's key to the amount of time we spend in our holding pattern, as well as the ability to be a blessing to others from experiences learned along the way. We are amazingly blessed because we get through the storms of this life when God's got our backs. When thinking about that last statement, we can find great relief and even a little joy in it. In Psalm 27:14, David rightfully reminds us to "Wait for the Lord; be strong and take heart and wait for the Lord."

Yes, Tommy, I would agree that waiting is definitely the hardest part, but it can also yield the greatest blessings.

15

Breaking Strongholds

"Jesus Christ is the same yesterday, and today, and forever"
(Hebrews 13:8).

I must be honest with you. I cannot imagine how anyone, especially nowadays, can have hope without knowing the Lord or relying on Him. I personally can't get through a day without total dependence on the assurance of His love and unfailing grace. The days grow darker with each passing hour as the enemy of our soul increases his attacks to try to distract us and keep us off God's course. He's working overtime because he knows his time is growing short. We know how the story ends, according to the book of Revelation. We win, and he loses. We know trials and temptations will come at us, sometimes from every side and often seemingly all at once. As quoted in John 16:33 (AMP), "I have told you these things, so that in Me you may have [perfect] peace. In the world you have tribulation and distress and suffering, but be courageous [be confident, be undaunted, be filled with joy]; I have overcome the world. [My conquest is accomplished, My victory abiding.]" Jesus, Himself, has told us to be cheerful because he has already "overcome the world." The devil is a liar and is defeated, though he will do his best to keep us distracted and out of God's will for our lives. That's when we decide to dig our heels in deeper, refusing to allow the enemy to cross the line we have drawn in the sand against him and remain anchored to Jesus, the lover of our soul.

I am convinced, without a shadow of a doubt, that evil paranormal phenomenon surrounds us on a daily basis. Supernaturally dysfunctional demonic dominions, as previously stated, are working overtime to keep us oppressed, depressed, distracted, and self-absorbed. They will do everything within their power to try to keep our focus on the problems of this world instead of the Lord. They are very good at their jobs and have been studying us for ages. They know what buttons to push to upset us and keep us off track with God's purpose for our lives. If you are predisposed to these attacks due to open doors from familial bloodline curses, you may have had years of these types of attacks through no fault of your own. You may be wondering, "So, where do I go from here? What do I do now?" Well, my friend, I'd like to end this book with hope-filled Scripture and declarations to equip you to fight the enemy, discern his tactics, and overcome all strongholds he's proclaimed over your life. He is actually afraid of you, especially when you learn how to use your God-given authority over him.

As a believer, you have the right to every single promise that is recorded in the Bible. If you've accepted Jesus Christ as your Lord and Savior, all of God's promises for you are "Yes and Amen" (2 Corinthians 1:20). You have a blood-bought right to all His promises, as well as authority over the enemy (Luke 10:19), through the shedding of the blood of Jesus on the cross. If you aren't sure that you are saved and would like to be, please pause for a moment, search your heart, and say this prayer when you are ready: "Dear Jesus, I humbly come before You this moment and ask Your forgiveness of all of my sins both known and unknown. I believe that You died for me and ask that You come into my heart. I accept You as my Savior and thank You for Your unending grace. In Jesus' name, I pray. Amen." It's a simple little prayer that packs a punch and can change your destiny in an instant. If you said it from the heart, you are now officially in the family of God and therefore entitled to all the best that God has for you. It's the most important decision you could ever make.

In chapter 10 of Romans, we are told, "That if you confess with your mouth, 'Jesus is Lord,' and believe in your heart that God raised him from the dead, you will be saved. For it is with your heart that you believe and are justified, and it is with your mouth that you confess and are saved" (Romans 10:9-10). If you prayed the above prayer, this scripture includes you. You are forgiven just as if you had never sinned. In 2 Corinthians, Paul explains, "Therefore if anyone is in Christ, he is a new creation; the old has gone, the new has come" (2 Corinthians 5:17). You are forgiven, highly favored, and ready to supernaturally arm yourself against the attacks of the enemy.

Ephesians explains that we are to "Finally, be strong in the Lord and in his mighty power. Put on the full armor of God so that you can take your stand against the devil's schemes" (Ephesians 6:10-11). I believe we need to read and speak aloud certain scriptures and declarations to properly spiritually arm ourselves and even impose counter-attacks on the devil and the demonic. We are clearly told, "For the word of God is alive and active. Sharper than any double-edged sword, it penetrates even to dividing soul and spirit, joints and marrow; it judges the thoughts and attitudes of the heart" (Hebrews 4:12). We are specifically instructed to use God's living Word as our number one line of defense in battling our enemy. This scripture in Hebrews confirms to us that God's Word is alive and sharper than a sword, which means when we speak God's Word, we have the power He has freely given us to overcome the oppressor.

I have found it extremely beneficial to not only quote the Bible out loud but also to personalize it while doing so. For example, a declaration for the above scripture might be, "Lord, I am claiming Ephesians 6:10 as my own. Therefore, I will be strong in You and in Your mighty power. I am dressing in Your full armor so that I can stand and overcome the devil's schemes against me and my family, in Jesus' name. Amen." I'd like to emphasize that I read the scripture as printed in its entirety and then may insert my, or my family member's, name as I declare its promise over our lives. For me, it makes His Word more personal to my specific circumstances and vocally tells the enemy that I'm on to him and done with his antics.

Your words contain power, especially when spoken aloud and backed by God's living Word, the Bible. "The tongue has the power of life and death, and those who love it will eat its fruit" (Proverbs 18:21). This scripture proves to us that our power-packed words make a difference in our current condition, especially when spoken. This scripture tells us the majorly huge importance of our words. If we speak out life-giving, healthy words towards ourselves, our situations, or others, we will reap living benefits. Likewise, if we continually speak negatively over ourselves or our challenges, we will reap extremely negative consequences, including death. We give the devil a foothold or open another one of those unwanted doors, helping him out even further by complaining about our circumstances or uttering words of unbelief. Negativity invites him in, period. That doesn't mean we act as if everything is Pollyanna perfect when our world seems to be crashing down all around us. We don't deny the reality of the moment, but we don't sacrifice the victory in our future by negative words that inhibit its manifestation. I cannot emphasize this point enough. You will become what you speak into being. Why not cling to God's Word and speak His promises regarding your supernatural inheritance instead of wallowing in the seemingly dark but soon-to-be-changing season that you may be in?

"All scripture is God-breathed and is useful for teaching, rebuking, correcting and training in righteousness," according to 2 Timothy 3:16. Since all scripture in the Bible is "God-breathed," alive and sharper than any two-edged sword, why not use it on a daily basis? His Word gives us life, energy, wisdom, and hope. It leads to divine healing in every single area of our lives when applied daily. Since every good and perfect thing comes from a heavenly Father who loves us, His Bible is the ultimate roadmap to our supernatural wholeness and happiness. The devil doesn't want you to know this and will send as many demonic obstacles as possible to keep you out of God's perfect will, Word, and purpose for your life. You need to be armed and battle-ready by using God's written words for any and every circumstance you may have to come against.

So, we now know we must open our mouths and shout at the devil since God unceasingly has our backs, as proven by the Scriptures He's already equipped us with. We don't have to be afraid with the creator of the universe on our side. With God's help, bloodline curses can most definitely be broken. In Proverbs, God explains, "Like a fluttering sparrow or a darting swallow, an undeserved curse does not come to rest" (Proverbs 26:2). Though we may possibly be pre-disposed to the ill effects of bloodline curses, they can't come to stay. The demonic and all curses have to flee or cease in the name of Jesus. You have the authority to proclaim and receive this Proverbs' scripture as your own when you are a spirit-filled believing child of God.

Besides, "Christ redeemed us from the curse of the law by becoming a curse for us, for it is written: 'Cursed is everyone who is hung on a tree'" (Galatians 3:13). The enemy's rights over you, through the dispatching of bloodline curses, ended when they crucified Jesus so long ago. He bore all our curses while He hung, dying on that cross. He did it of His own free will because of His love for each one of us. We cannot afford to take His sacrifice for granted. If we live in defeat, bound by any type of bloodline or self-induced curse, it's as though we are slapping Him in the face and unappreciative of all He's done for us. I've grieved the Lord enough in my past. I refuse to lay down and stay bound by a defeated foe when Jesus Himself gave me all the tools and power necessary to overcome him once and for all. I've decided to stand firm and fight the good fight of faith (1 Timothy 6:12) for as long as the Lord gives me breath.

God said in Genesis 27:29, "I will bless those who bless you, and whoever curses you I will curse." Your declaration using this scripture could be something along the lines of "Lord, I stand on the promise You gave me in Genesis 27:29 that You will bless those who bless me and will curse whoever tries to curse me. That includes any bloodline curse that may try to attach itself to me or my family. I denounce and break any tie the devil claims to have over us and claim the blood of Jesus over any and all curses attacking our lives. In the name of Jesus, I receive your promise. Thank You, Lord. Amen." Again, there is no tried-and-true formula that magically makes God show up and conquer the enemy for us. We already have all that we need within us to overcome the devil because Christ lives in us (Colossians 1:27). He died to set us free from the curse of the law, as well as all bloodline curses. You don't have to put your name in Scripture exactly as I do. You can simply come to God any time in prayer, read His Word, and arm yourself against the enemy's attacks

SUPERNATURALLY DYSFUNCTIONAL

by using your own words to claim His promises as your own. You can cry out to Him from whatever is welling up within your own heart. He will whisper words of wisdom when you seek Him with your whole heart. You will uncover divine revelation by simply spending time with Him in His Word. You could also actually be delivered from any type of curse the enemy has thrown your way. Unafraid, unashamed, and destined to divine victory in the Lord. Now that's an encouraging legacy to look forward to! You deserve a curse-broken future filled with God's promises of hope! That is my wish for you. To truly know who you are in Christ. You are more than a conqueror, according to Romans 8:37! Believe it!

I'd like to declare Isaiah 54 over you: "I declare that no weapon forged against you _____, will prevail, and you _____, will refute every tongue that accuses you. This is the heritage of _____, the servant of the Lord, and this is their vindication from me," declares the Lord. (Isaiah 54:17). We declare and believe to receive the promise of this scripture for _____ in Jesus' name. Amen.

Let's agree and declare Matthew 16 together for you as well: "I will give you _____, the keys of the kingdom of heaven; whatever you _____ bind on earth will be bound in heaven, and whatever you _____ loose on earth will be loosed in heaven." Lord, we bind all bloodline curses that are coming against _____ in Jesus' name. We believe that as we bind the curses, the enemy is attacking _____ with on earth, that You are binding them in heaven as well. Lord, we now loose all Your blessings over _____ on the earth as we believe _____'s blessings will be loosed in heaven according to Your Word. In the precious name of Jesus, we now declare and receive this scripture as our blood-bought right. Thank you, Lord. Amen.

Dear heavenly Father, we come boldly to Your throne in the name of Jesus Christ, our Lord and Savior. We thank You that since we are joint-heirs with Jesus, we have authority over the devil and all his demonic followers. Right now, Lord, we claim the blood of Jesus over all bloodline curses the devil has unleashed upon us individually as well as on our families. We take the authority You gave us when we joined Your family, over the supernatural powers of the prince of the air and this world, in Jesus' name.

Satan, we take great pleasure in commanding that you take your hands off our bodies and our families in Jesus' name! We declare you are under our feet as it says in Romans 16:20. You are defeated, an offense and abomination, and you no longer have a claim on our bodies or our families in Jesus' name! We command that you leave immediately and that no weapon formed against us will prosper in Jesus' name. We have bound you and your demons on earth, and you are therefore bound in heaven.

We rebuke you and strip you of all claims over us in Jesus' name! You no longer have any authority over our familial bloodlines from this moment on, and you must go now in the name above all names, Jesus! Devil, you are bound and done tormenting our families in Jesus' name! We claim the blood of Jesus over our bloodlines from this moment on, and you, devil, no longer have any claims on us or our families in Jesus' name!

We now claim Psalm 91 in its entirety over ourselves and our families and believe what it tells us in verse 4, "He will cover you with his feathers, and under his wings you will find refuge." Lord, we believe that You are loosing a hedge of protection around us and our families, especially as the devil tries to gain a stronghold in our lives. We believe that we will find protection under the shadow of Your wings and thank You for it, Lord, in Jesus' name. We are making You, dear heavenly Father, our dwelling place, and believe, as You told us in verse 10, that no harm will befall us or our families. We believe that You are commanding your angels to guard us and our loved ones for generations to come, in Jesus' name.

Lord, we stand on Your promise, as You stated in verse 14, that because we love You, You will rescue us and protect us as we acknowledge Your name. We are calling upon You, Father, and know You will answer us because You said You would. You promised You would be with us during our toughest times and that You would deliver us, and we believe You, Lord. We stand on Your promise in verse 16 that you will satisfy us with a long life and show us your salvation (Psalm 91). We believe that we are saved and will enjoy a long, healthy, and cursed-free life because of Your promises through Christ Jesus. We love You, Lord, and give You all the glory, honor, and praise forever, in Jesus' name. Amen.

16

Wired for Eternity

Every event in our lives has meaning. Everything, whether good or bad, brings about a chance for us to learn, overcome obstacles and ultimately bless others. That's our superpower, really, along with prayer. The human capacity to forgive and love is enormous. We were put on this earth right here, right now, to leave our salty and dysfunctionally unique and personal mark on it. We were designed to make a difference in the lives of all we encounter. The bumps along the path of our journey only slow us down; they aren't meant to stop us completely. God loves you too much to allow that to happen. All challenges can be good when we grow and learn from them. Perhaps the bumps and bruises allow us the ability to help or encourage others who have had to suffer the same. We are blessed because we have gone through the storms of life and made it to the other side, where healing begins. We are blessed to be a blessing as we share what God has done for us with those who desperately need to hear our story.

We now understand that the enemy is often the true culprit behind evil-intending supernatural attacks, manifestations, and challenges that inhibit our goals and challenge our beliefs. We also know that we are more than conquerors and equipped with all we need to overcome his tactics and beat him at his games. So, what are we waiting for? We know that God can turn all that the enemy meant for evil into something amazingly good. We can be used to further God's kingdom by being willing vessels to spread the great good news of His unwavering love for us all. He wants us to be wholehearted, all in, and supernaturally functional every single day of our lives. We are wired for an eternity with Him, which as our ultimate "end game" result, is a truly encouraging thought.

The ball is in your court, my friend. It's up to you to make a choice to use that God-given superpower within you, to rise up, take a stand against the enemy of your soul, and dare to hope and trust in the Lord. He's got this, and so do you!

Bibliography

Faithwords, AMP, The Holy Bible, New York: Faith Words, 2018.

King James Bible (2020). *King James Bible Online,* Original work published 1769. <www.kingjamesbibleonline.org>.

Zondervan, NIV, The Holy Bible, Grand Rapids, Michigan: Zondervan, 1984.

"Dictionary.com." 2021 <www.dictionary.com>

"Wikipedia." 2021 <www.en.wikipedia.org>.

"National Institute of Health." 2021 <www.healthline.com>

"Merriam Webster: An Encyclopedia Britannica Company." 2021 <www.merriamwebster.com>

About the Author

Stephanie has been fascinated by the supernatural for as long as she can remember. Personal encounters, as well as familial testimonials, lead to an extensive research into her family history.

Though the uncovering of bloodline curses overwhelmed the entire family, she was amazed to find God's presence in tangible ways every step of the way, fueling her desire to share all that He has done with those who desperately need to hear it.

Stephanie is a wife, mother of four grown children, a Naturopathic Doctor, and a holistic wellness coach. She is currently RVing her way across the country with her husband, Jon, along with their two dogs, Thor and Loki.

For more information, questions, or comments, you may contact her at sewoodynd.wordpress.com or sewoody16@gmail.com.